P9-CRZ-829

Edgar Allan Poe:

Tales and Poems

~∞∾Writers and Their Works∾∞~

Edgar Allan Poe:
Tales and Poems

RAYCHEL HAUGRUD REIFF

Marshall Cavendish
Benchmark
New York

With thanks to Paul Grimstad, assistant professor of English at Yale University,
for his expert review of this manuscript.

Marshall Cavendish Benchmark
99 White Plains Road
Tarrytown, NY 10591
www.marshallcavendish.us

All quotations are cited in the text. Additional information and sources
are included in the Notes section of this book.

Library of Congress Cataloging-in-Publication Data

Reiff, Raychel Haugrud.
Edgar Allan Poe : tales and poems / by Raychel Haugrud Reiff.
p. cm. — (Writers and their works)
Includes bibliographical references and index.
Summary: "A biography of writer Edgar Allan Poe that describes his era, his major works, and the
legacy of his writing"—Provided by publisher.
ISBN 978-0-7614-2963-0
1. Poe, Edgar Allan, 1809–1849. 2. Authors, American—19th century—Biography. I. Title.
PS2631.R42 2008
818'.309—dc22

2007035662

Photo Research by Lindsay Aveilhe and Linda Sykes Picture Research, Inc.

Cover photo: The Granger Collection

The photographs in this book are used by permission and through the courtesy of:
The Granger Collection: 2, 25, 39, 47, 50, 66; Special Collections, University of Virginia Library: 10,
14, 22; John Henry Ingram's Poe Collection, MSS 38-135, Special Collections, University of Virginia
Library: 17; Mary Evans Picture Library: 29, 82; Historic Buildings Survey/The Library
of Congress (HABS PA 1735-1): 32; istockphoto.com: 35; Antar Dayal Illustration Works/Corbis: 45;
Woolaroc Museum, OK/Peter Newark Western Americana/The Bridgeman Art Library: 54;
Blue Lantern Studio/Corbis: 58; Hulton Archive/Getty Images: 74; Library of Congress: 97;
Universal/The Kobal Collection: 109.

Publisher: Michelle Bisson
Art Director: Anahid Hamparian
Series Designer: Sonia Chagbatzanian

Printed in Malaysia
1 3 5 6 4 2

Table of Contents

lled with fear, he tells himself that some visitor has
d opens the door. When no one appears, he imagines
nore may have knocked and whispers her name, hearing
echo murmuring back. Returning to his chamber, he
ain hears the tapping, this time louder. Assuming it is
nd rattling his door, he opens a shutter, and a sta
ven steps into his chamber and perches on the bust of Pa
ove his chamber door. When he asks its name, the r
plies, "Nevermore." The lonely poet thinks that the ra
ke his other friends, will soon leave, but the raven s
evermore." Suddenly, he hears a tapping at his chamber d
though filled with fear, he tells himself that some vis
s come and opens the door. When no one appears, he imag
at Lenore may have knocked and whispers her name, hea
ly an echo murmuring back. Returning to his chamber
ce again hears the tapping, this time louder. Assuming
e wind rattling his door, he opens a shutter, and a sta
ven steps into his chamber and perches on the bust of Pa
ove his chamber door. When he asks its name, the r
plies, "Nevermore." The lonely poet thinks that the ra
ke his other friends, will soon leave, but the raven s
evermore." Suddenly, he hears a tapping at his chamber d
though filled with fear, he tells himself that some vis
s come and opens the door. When no one appears, he imag
at Lenore may have knocked and whispers her name, hea
ly an echo murmuring back. Returning to his chamber
ce again hears the tapping, this time louder. Assuming
e wind rattling his door, he opens a shutter, and a sta
ven steps into his chamber and perches on the bust of Pa
ove his chamber door. When he asks its name, the r
plies, "Nevermore." The lonely poet thinks that the ra
ke his other friends, will soon leave, but the raven s
evermore." Suddenly, he hears a tapping at his chamber d
though filled with fear, he tells himself that some vis
s come and opens the door. When no one appears, he imag
at Lenore may have knocked and whispers her name, hea
ly an echo murmuring back. Returning to his chamber
ce again hears the tapping, this time louder. Assuming
e wind rattling his door, he opens a shutter, and a sta
ven steps into his chamber and perches on the bust of Pa
ove his chamber door. When he asks its name, the r
plies, "Nevermore." The lonely poet thinks that the ra

Introduction

EDGAR POE was born in Boston, Massachusetts, in 1809 to actor parents. An orphan before his third birthday, Edgar was raised by John and Frances Allan of Richmond, Virginia, and used their surname as his middle name even though he was not formally adopted. First educated in England and Virginia, he received his higher education at the University of Virginia and in the military. Poe had a short, hard life. After being cast out of his foster parents' home over quarrels about money at the age of eighteen, Poe tried to earn a living as a writer at a time when it was impossible to do so in America; he was impoverished the rest of his life. To make enough money to live, Poe worked as an editor, critic, journalist, lecturer, and freelance writer. He broke into the U.S. literary field as a teenager, publishing his first book of poems when he was eighteen. During the next two decades, he was recognized as a major figure in three types of American literature—the short story, poetry, and criticism. In the short story, Poe is admired for his masterpieces of death, horror, evil, and perversity, and also for his detective stories. His poems, including one of the most famous poems in the English language, "The Raven," show his expert command of poetic language and rhythms. As a literary critic, Poe was one of the first to advocate for standards by which to judge literary works, and he set forth a definition of the short story that is still used today.

In 1849, at age forty, Poe mysteriously died in Baltimore, Maryland, where he was found unconscious on the street. His literary executor, Rufus Wilmot Griswold, immediately spewed out his hatred for the dead author by writing memoirs filled with half-truths and falsehoods that cast Poe as an immoral drunkard and addict. Poe named Griswold his literary executor not knowing that the man, who appeared to be his friend, harbored intense hatred for him; Griswold was the Iago to Poe's Othello. Because of what Griswold wrote, Poe's personal reputation was ruined. As a person, he is still generally regarded as a bad or weak man—a psychotic alcoholic and drug abuser. Nevertheless, he is recognized today as the undisputed master of the American Gothic horror story, the inventor of the modern detective story, one of the distinctive voices of poetry, and a distinguished critic.

Chapter 1

The Life of Edgar Allan Poe

AS A YOUTH, HE DREAMED OF BEING a published author and was disappointed when his foster father refused to pay for the printing of a volume of poems. His dream became a reality when, at age eighteen, he was thrown out of his well-to-do home in Virginia without food, clothes, or money. The aspiring writer made his way to Boston and succeeded in getting his book, *Tamerlane and Other Poems*, published in June 1827. This very plain, small book was hardly noticed; it was not reviewed by any press. Of the fifty printed copies, only a few sold, and for merely twelve and a half cents each (Haining, 9). At that time, no one would have guessed that the author, simply called "A Bostonian," would one day be renowned as a literary legend: the genius named Edgar Allan Poe.

Although today his works are well known, his life is not. Indeed, many of the facts of Edgar Allan Poe's life and personality have been misunderstood or misinterpreted. The major problems of understanding this man stem from two sources. The first comes from a memoir full of lies and half-truths about Poe written by Rufus Griswold, a spiteful fellow author who almost single-handedly destroyed Poe's reputation by casting him as a type of devil—an irredeemable alcoholic and drug addict with an inherently immoral nature. Until recently, most biographers relied on the false Griswold portrait of Poe as the true picture of the man. The second problem is that biographers have often analyzed Poe's personality by examining his tales of horror, madness, terror, murders, and deaths. Incorrectly identifying the writer with his melancholic, sick, psychotic narrators, they have tended to look

THE YOUNG, PENNILESS EDGAR ALLAN POE WOULD HAVE THOUGHT HE WAS DREAMING, INDEED, HAD HE KNOWN THAT HIS WRITING WOULD LEAD NOT JUST TO FAME BUT TO ARTISTIC IMMORTALITY.

upon Poe as a "gifted psychopath describing with consummate artistry his personal instabilities and abnormalities. Hence the idea—old, persistent and widespread—that the somber figure of Edgar Allan Poe stalks forever through the pages of his stories and poems" (Buranelli, 18).

Adding to the confusion are some details about the writer that cannot be proven. No birth certificate has been found, which leads to questions about the date and place of his birth; some years are missing in Poe's life; Poe's activities during his last days are unknown; the cause of his death is undocumented; and the location and date of his burial are questionable. In addition, Poe himself changed a few facts of his life to help create a public image that would enhance his reputation and help sell his works. He made up events, such as joining the Greeks in their fight for independence (Lowell, 7), and he invented relatives, for example, claiming that he was the grandson of Benedict Arnold (Gibson, 52).

However, in recent years, a clearer picture of the life and personality of this remarkable writer and man has emerged.

Childhood: 1809-1827

Edgar Poe was born on January 19, 1809, in Boston. His parents, Elizabeth (Eliza) Arnold Hopkins Poe and David Poe Jr., loved the theater, and both worked as professional actors even though such jobs offered no financial or job security. Eliza was an industrious woman who had come from England with her actress mother when she was nine years old. She began appearing on stage that year and probably started acting professionally when she was orphaned at eleven. From then until her death, this pretty, charming, talented actress was in high demand. After her first husband, Charles Hopkins, died in 1805, Eliza married David Poe Jr., a handsome, petulant, and probably hard-drinking young man from Baltimore who had quit law school at age nineteen to become an actor, much to the displeasure of his family. Although not considered as talented as his wife, David Poe was constantly employed.

The two settled in Boston for three years where they both worked tirelessly to establish themselves as actors. The Poes had three children: William Henry (called Henry), born January 30, 1807; Edgar, born two years later; and Rosalie, born in the fall or winter of 1810. Ten months after Edgar's birth, David Poe stopped acting. Some biographers, including Kenneth Silverman, think he abandoned his family (*Edgar A. Poe*, 7), but others, such as Arthur Hobson Quinn, suggest that he may have remained with his family, leaving Eliza Poe to struggle valiantly with "the care of a husband, either an invalid or out of work, and of her two children" (39). Though he disappeared in late 1809, before Rosalie was born, no one knows where David Poe went, what became of him, or when he died.

In the summer of 1811, poverty-stricken Eliza was sick, possibly of an infectious fever, and on December 8, 1811, with her small children by her side, Poe's twenty-four-year-old mother died in Richmond, Virginia. She left little Edgar a locket containing a miniature painting of her, a gift he preserved throughout his life. Eliza Poe also passed on to her son "her high heart, her unremitting industry, and that indefinable charm that made her a favorite from Boston to Charleston among the theatre-goers of that day" (A. H. Quinn, 1). Although he was only a toddler when his mother died, Edgar must have been strongly affected by her death, as well as from his separation from his brother and sister after her death, as evidenced by the fearful attitude toward loss and death in many of his writings.

Henry, not quite five, was sent to Baltimore to live with his grandparents, David Poe Sr. and his wife, Elizabeth Cairnes Poe. Baby Rosalie was adopted by the William

Mackenzie family of Richmond, and Edgar, not quite three, became the foster son of a prominent Richmond couple, John and Frances Allan, who, although they had no legal obligation or contract, promised Poe's grandparents that they would give Edgar a liberal education.

Edgar's life changed dramatically when he went to live with wealthy John Allan, a partner in the firm Ellis and Allan, merchants and exporters of tobacco and other goods. Materially, young Edgar had everything he could desire—a beautiful home with gilt chairs, engravings, a flute, and a pianoforte; three slaves; a carriage; dining tables overflowing with herring, ham, venison, and chocolates; and an ample supply of liquors—brandy, rum, whisky, and gin (Silverman, *Edgar A. Poe*, 11, 13–14). Emotionally, however, things were probably less fulfilling.

John Allan, whom Edgar called "Pa" even though Allan never legally adopted him, was not a very loving father. Silverman describes him as a "sharp, hard-working merchant whose sententious [pompous] moralism bespoke his rigorous and resentful demands on personal conduct" although he "could be charitable and relaxed" (14). Frances (Fanny) Allan, whom Edgar called "Ma," seems to have had more sympathy and love for the little child. But, prone to accidents and illnesses her family believed were imaginary, she often had no time for her ward. The Allans enjoyed an active social life, and they raised little Edgar as a well-bred Southern gentleman.

Edgar began his education in Europe when he was six and a half. In 1815, the Allan family moved to London where John Allan relocated to expand his business. The young boy, now called Edgar Allan, was sent to expensive boarding schools where he excelled in his studies, especially French, Latin, history, and literature. One of his teachers described Edgar as "a quick and clever boy and would have been a very good boy if he had not been spoilt by his parents, . . . but they spoilt him, and allowed him

JOHN ALLEN AGREED TO RAISE THE YOUNG WRITER-TO-BE, BUT HE DID NOT PROMISE TO GIVE HIM AFFECTION.

an extravagant amount of pocket-money, which enabled him to get into all manner of mischief" (quoted in A. H. Quinn, 71–72). Not surprisingly, the little orphan was often lonely at a boarding school away from his caretakers. John Allan, busy with work, had little time for his family, and Fanny was often sick and bedridden. After five years, John Allan's business failed, and the family returned to Richmond in 1820 when Edgar was eleven.

In Virginia, Edgar was well-liked by other boys. Thomas Ellis, the son of Allan's business partner, greatly admired him as a leader and a friend: "No boy ever had a greater influence over me than he had. He was, indeed, a leader among boys; but my admiration for him scarcely knew bounds. . . . He taught me to shoot, to swim, and to skate, to play bandy, &c.; and I ought to mention that he once saved me from drowning—for having thrown me into the falls headlong, that I might strike out for myself, he presently found it necessary to come to my help, or it would have been too late" (quoted in A. H. Quinn, 82).

In spite of financial troubles, Allan continued to send Edgar to school in Richmond, where he was now called Edgar Poe. Here he once again demonstrated a gift for language, excelling in Latin and French. His teacher, Joseph H. Clarke, regarded him highly, describing him as "playful," "remarkable for self-respect, without haughtiness," "strictly just and correct in his demeanor with his fellow playmates," possessing "an enthusiastic ardor in everything he undertook," "tenacious" and unyielding when he had a difference of opinion, "ambitious to excel," having "a sensitive and tender heart," and filled with great "imaginative powers" (quoted in A. H. Quinn, 83). As a teenager, Edgar already loved to write verses and wanted to have them published. The most common way to do this was to self-publish, but Allan refused to pay for this. Besides being a scholar, Edgar excelled in athletics as a runner, leaper, boxer, and especially a swimmer. He was also a leader, becoming, at age fifteen, a lieutenant of the Junior Morgan Riflemen, a volunteer company of Richmond boys (Silverman, *Edgar A. Poe*, 24–25).

Because Fanny Allan was often sick and could do little mothering, Edgar looked for other mother figures. When he was fourteen, he formed an attachment to Jane Stanard, the thirty-year-old mother of a classmate. Devoted to her, he wrote his first poem, titled "To Helen," to this woman, who, according to Poe's aunt, "consoled and comforted him" when he "was unhappy at home (which was often the case)" (quoted in A. H. Quinn, 86). When she died a year later, the heartbroken boy often visited her grave and wept upon it. At home, he was sad and crabby, leading John Allan to think he was thankless, complaining to Henry Poe in 1824, "The boy possesses not a Spark of affection for us not a particle of gratitude for all my care and kindness towards him" (Thomas and Jackson, 61).

Besides being frustrated with his ward, Allan continued to have financial troubles, which forced him to quit his partnership with Ellis in 1824. Unexpectedly, his wealthy uncle, William Galt, died in 1825 and left Allan a huge inheritance. The Allans moved to a splendid home near the James River. About this time, Edgar became interested in a local fifteen-year-old girl named Elmira Royster, and the two became engaged.

In February 1826, Edgar enrolled at the University of Virginia, a newly constructed school with few rules and little discipline. Here life was difficult for the seventeen-year-old even though he had many successes—excelling in his studies, particularly Latin and French; becoming recognized as a great debater and an outstanding athlete; and entertaining friends with his poetry. For one thing, he was lonely, cut off from friends and family. His foster father visited him only once during his year at school, and his fiancée did not answer his letters. (Unknown to him,

FRANCES "FANNY" ALLAN WAS MORE LOVING TOWARD EDGAR THAN
HER HUSBAND, BUT SHE WAS OFTEN TOO ILL TO PAY MUCH ATTENTION
TO THE BOY.

Elmira's father, who opposed their engagement because of their youth, intercepted those letters.) A second reason for Edgar's unhappiness was that he was frightened by the violent atmosphere at the university. Silverman writes that "during Edgar's year, seven students were suspended or expelled for high-stakes gambling, assaults, or drunkenness. . . . One of his schoolmates, drunk on mint-sling and down about two hundred dollars at cards, accused another player of cheating and whipped him with a cowhide strap. Several scholars besieged the house of a townsman and stripped the clothes off his servant-woman, believing she had 'infected the Students with disease'" (*Edgar A. Poe*, 31).

Edgar was also unhappy because he was plagued with money problems. For some reason, John Allan did not give him enough money to pay for his board, books, and personal expenses, and Poe immediately fell into debt. Biographer Arthur Hobson Quinn sympathizes with Poe for the "almost incredible meanness" of John Allan, who "deliberately, without a decent allowance, or even the minimum charges of the institution" sent Poe to college. Quinn says, "Allan was in easy circumstances, and yet he refused to contribute for a year's expenses less than a third of the amount he had paid in England when he was not by any means so well off" (113).

In order to pay his debts, Edgar resorted to gambling, which caused him even greater problems. After one year, he returned to Richmond because Allan refused to pay his debts or support him for another term at the university. Adding to Poe's disappointment, Elmira Royster was now engaged to someone else. In March 1827, Edgar, needing money to pay his creditors, had a two-day fight with John Allan, who threw his foster son out of his house. The eighteen-year-old's letters to Allan begging him to send him his clothes and some money for food and lodging did not soften Allan's heart. Edgar—homeless, starving, harassed by creditors, and untrained for any profession—left Richmond and disappeared for a couple of months. To escape creditors, he sometimes used an alias and spread rumors that he had gone to sea (Silverman, *Edgar A. Poe*, 37).

Military Life: 1827-1831

Poe is next heard of around June 1827, when a small book of poems, *Tamerlane and Other Poems*, appeared, its anonymous author called "a Bostonian." The book brought Poe no money and no critical attention. Desperate, Poe enlisted for a five-year term in the U.S. Army as a private soldier, calling himself Edgar A. Perry. Here he once again distinguished himself for his excellent work and exemplary habits, and, in 1829, was promoted to the rank of sergeant major, the highest rank for non-commissioned officers. After two years, he wanted to leave the army, and he penitently wrote to his foster father to ask him to use his influence to help him get into the United States Military Academy at West Point as a cadet, which Allan finally agreed to do. The two men were briefly reconciled when Fanny Allan died on February 28, 1829. Honorably discharged from the army in April 1829, Poe was relatively happy.

Getting into West Point took a long time, and Poe, living in Baltimore with no income, sought financial support from Allan, which caused new quarrels between them. At the end of the year, Poe pitifully wrote to Allan, "I wrote you about a fortnight ago and as I have not heard from you, I was afraid you had forgotten me—I would not trouble you so often if I was not extremely pinched—I am almost without clothes—and, as I board by the month, the lady with whom I board is anxious for [her] money" (*Letters*, Vol. 1, 33). Allan did send Poe some money but soon told his ward, "I am not particularly anxious to see you" (quoted in Silverman, *Edgar A. Poe*, 52), which, to Poe, meant he should not return home.

While waiting to get into the military academy, Poe worked at getting his poetry published in magazines. In September, when "Fairy-Land" appeared in the *Yankee and Boston Literary Gazette*, the young poet was cheered by the editor's comments that the author "might make a beautiful and perhaps a magnificent poem. There is a good deal here to justify such a hope" (Neal, 3). By the end of the year, Poe had succeeded in getting *Al Aaraaf, Tamerlane, and Minor Poems* published, identifying himself as "Edgar A. Poe," the way he signed all of his subsequent works.

Finally, in 1830, Poe was admitted to West Point, where, once again, he excelled as a scholar, particularly in linguistics and mathematics. But life did not go well for young Poe because Allan refused to give him the financial support expected for all cadets. Allan was furious with his ward because of an unflattering letter about him that Poe had written to Sergeant Samuel "Bully" Graves, the man who had taken Poe's place in the army. Although Poe owed Graves money for this favor, he could not give him any because, he explained to Graves, Allan was "not very often sober" and "shuffles me off" (*Letters*, Vol. 1, 36). Allan had also started a new family, remarrying in fall 1830. Poe, seeing no future as a low-paid officer and unable to resign without his guardian's permission, which Allan refused to give, intentionally violated the academy's rules by being absent from parades and roll calls and by not attending classes. He was dismissed in February 1831.

New York and Baltimore: 1831-1834

From now on, Poe was determined to be a professional writer. Throughout his adult life, he lived in four of America's largest cities—Baltimore; Richmond, Virginia; New York; and Philadelphia—working as an editor of literary magazines, writing critiques of literature, and authoring poetry, short stories, and a novel. Although he was a brilliant editor and an extraordinarily gifted writer, he could not make a living from his work. No matter how hard he toiled, no matter what prizes he won, no matter how many superb tales and exquisite poems he produced, Poe could not make enough money to live comfortably in early nineteenth-century America. He continually suffered from extreme poverty, overwork, tension, and disappointment.

After he left West Point, Poe moved to New York City, where he almost immediately became ill. Although he begged Allan, "Please send me a little money," because he had "no money—no friends . . . besides a most violent cold on my lungs my *ear* discharges blood and matter continuall[y]" (*Letters*, Vol. 1, 44, 43), his foster father did not respond to his desperate appeal. At the end of April, Poe's new volume of poetry was published. *Poems by Edgar A. Poe . . . Second Edition* was dedicated to his classmates at West Point who had raised money to publish this book.

About this same time, Poe moved to Baltimore and joined the household of his impoverished Aunt Maria (Muddy) Poe Clemm. Also living with her were his grandmother; his brother, William Henry Poe; and Muddy's children, eight-year-old Virginia (Sissy) and Henry Clemm. At last, he had a family that unconditionally loved him. His relationship with his brother, with whom he felt a strong tie, did not last long because Henry, an alcoholic, died on August 1, 1831 (Silverman, *Edgar A. Poe*, 85).

Not much is known of Poe's life for the next three years. After trying unsuccessfully to get a position as a teacher, he seems to have struggled to support himself and his family as a freelance writer, creating short stories when his poetry did not earn him enough money. Never idle, Poe was described by his friend, Lambert Wilmer, as "one of the most hardworking men in the world" who was

EDGAR ALLAN POE'S AUNT MUDDY PROVIDED A HAVEN FOR THE YOUNG MAN FOR A TIME AFTER HE LEFT WEST POINT.

always carefully dressed as an honorable gentleman. Wilmer relates: "I never saw him in any dress which was not fashionably neat, with some approximation to elegance. Indeed I often wondered how he could contrive to equip himself so handsomely, considering that his pecuniary resources were generally scanty and precarious enough" (quoted in A. H. Quinn, 197).

When the *Philadelphia Saturday Courier* offered a prize for the best short story, Poe sent in five. Although none won the prize, they were all printed in the *Courier* in 1832. They appeared anonymously, and it seems unlikely that Poe was paid for any of these tales. A Gothic tale of revenge, "Metzengerstein," appeared in January 1832, and four comic tales followed: "The Duc de L'Omelette," "A Tale of Jerusalem," "A Decided Loss," and "The Bargain Lost." The following year, he won a fifty-dollar prize from the *Baltimore Saturday Visitor* for his short story "MS. Found in a Bottle," a story of horror on the ocean. Poe became a lifelong friend of one of the *Visitor*'s judges, John Pendleton Kennedy, a lawyer and a writer who helped Poe financially, aided him in getting his works published, and got him his first editorial job.

The prize money was urgently needed by the family, as seen by the desperate letter Poe wrote to Allan in April 1833: "without friends, without any means, consequently of obtaining employment, I am perishing—absolutely perishing for want of aid. And yet I am not idle—nor addicted to any vice—nor have I committed any offence against society which would render me deserving of so hard a fate. For God's sake pity me, and save me from destruction" (*Letters*, Vol. 1, 49–50). Allan did not answer and refused to use his influence to help Poe get a job.

In early 1834, Poe, learning that John Allan was ill, rushed to Richmond to see him. Against the wishes of Allan's wife, Poe hurried to his guardian's bedroom, but Allan raised his cane, threatening to strike the young man. On March 27, John Allan died, leaving no mention of his ward in his will.

Poe continued to slave on his short stories and published eleven of them before leaving Baltimore.

Richmond: 1835-1837

With no hope of an inheritance and unable to live on the income from his writing, Poe, "now in a state of starvation," according to Kennedy (quoted in Silverman, *Edgar A. Poe*, 102), accepted a job as an editor of the *Southern Literary Messenger* in Richmond, Virginia, where he moved in August 1835. He planned to support his Aunt Muddy and cousin Virginia, who were badly in need of money because Grandmother Poe had died in July, and the family no longer received her $240 yearly pension as the widow of a war hero.

Family troubles immediately arose. Destitute Muddy wrote that Neilson Poe, a cousin, had offered a home to Virginia and possibly Muddy, an offer that meant Poe would lose both his cousin and the only real mother he had known. Although it is strange by today's standards, Poe, age twenty-six, had fallen in love with thirteen-year-old Virginia. Anguished, he wrote to Muddy, "My last my last my only hold on life is cruelly torn away—I have no desire to live and *will not*. . . . I love, *you know* I love Virginia passionately devotedly. . . . my agony is more than I can bear— . . . for love like mine can never be gotten over." To Virginia, he added a postscript: "My love, my own sweetest Sissy, my darling little wifey, thi[nk w]ell before you break the heart of your cousin. Eddy" (*Letters*, Vol. 1, 69–71). Almost immediately after receiving Muddy's letter, Poe left his job and hurried back to Baltimore. On September 22, he and Virginia got a marriage license, but they were not married until May 16, 1836 (A. H. Quinn, 227–228). They were first cousins,

EDGAR ALLAN POE FELL IN LOVE WITH HIS COUSIN, VIRGINIA, WHEN SHE WAS ONLY THIRTEEN YEARS OLD, AND MARRIED HER SHORTLY THEREAFTER. PEOPLE OFTEN MARRIED THEIR COUSINS IN THE NINE-TEENTH CENTURY, BUT THEY DIDN'T USUALLY MARRY SO YOUNG.

but marriage between such close relatives was not uncommon at the time. However, marrying a thirteen-year-old-girl *was* unusual.

In early October 1835, Poe got back his job at the *Messenger*, and he returned to Richmond with Muddy and Virginia. Poe was devoted to Virginia throughout his life, and she adored him. According to a friend, Poe committed "a large part of his salary to Virginia's education, and she was instructed in every elegant accomplishment at his expense." The friend explains that Poe "showed his affection in the right way, by endeavoring to make his companion happy. According to the opportunities he possessed, he supplied her with the comforts and luxuries of life. He kept a piano to gratify her taste for music, at a time when his income could scarcely afford such an indulgence. I never knew him to give her an unkind word, and doubt if they ever had any disagreement" (quoted in A. H. Quinn, 198).

Although he was not called the editor of the *Southern Literary Messenger*, Poe did all the editorial jobs, advising his boss on articles to publish, editing copy, requesting manuscripts, and writing reviews, fillers, fiction, poetry, and editorials. As a critic, Poe was, as Sidney P. Moss explains, "fundamentally a literary reformer, a rather lone figure on the American scene who, wanting to maintain a high literary tradition, waged a career-long war against those commercial forces that today have become all too conspicuous" (247–248). His literary critiques, in which he harshly faulted reviewers for unjustly praising mediocre works, produced both enthusiasm and debate, and Poe was seen as a type of warring American Indian who used a tomahawk to destroy others. In 1836 the Cincinnati *Mirror* admired Poe as an editor with "savage skill . . . [who] uses his tomahawk and scalping knife" to condemn bad writers, while other periodical critics claimed that "like an Indian, who cannot realize that an enemy is conquered till he is scalped," Poe went overboard in his denunciations (quoted in Silverman, *Edgar A. Poe*, 122). This image of being the man with a tomahawk clung to Poe for the rest of his life ("The Literary Mohawk," 79).

With an acute knowledge of the reading public and a strong business sense, Poe was the brilliant editor of the *Southern Literary Messenger* magazine from 1835 to 1837, miraculously raising its subscribers from fewer than one thousand to more than five thousand (Silverman, *Edgar A. Poe*, 127). However, relations between the publisher, Thomas W. White, and Poe became strained because White wanted more control of his magazine, and Poe was dissatisfied with both his low pay and his employer's lack of appreciation for his work and abilities. In January 1837, the publisher dismissed one of the best editors in America.

New York: 1837-1838

What Poe did for the next two and a half years is not known. Unemployed, poverty-stricken, and disillusioned, Poe almost disappeared from view. He, Virginia, and Muddy moved to America's publishing center, New York, for about a year, where, according to one of Poe's literary acquaintances, they lived "on bread and molasses for weeks together" (Thomas and Jackson, 248). In 1837, Poe published his only completed novel, *The Narrative of Arthur Gordon Pym*; however, the book brought him very little money even though the *New Yorker* critic wrote that the novel was "a work of extraordinary, freezing interest beyond anything we ever read. . . . Those who delight in the wonderful and horrible have a feast before them," and many agreed (quoted in Silverman, *Edgar A. Poe*, 137). Because there were no copyright laws, two pirated editions appeared in England, for which Poe received nothing.

Philadelphia: 1838-1843

With his financial situation so serious, Poe moved his family to another literary center, Philadelphia, in the summer of 1838. Here he published his well-regarded story, "Ligeia," for which he earned a paltry ten dollars (Silverman, *Edgar A. Poe*, 140). After a year in Philadelphia, Poe finally found employment in June 1839. He began working for William Evans Burton as an editor of *Burton's Gentleman's Magazine*, earning only ten dollars per week, or about five hundred dollars per year. At this time a customs director was paid an annual salary of about $1,200. As he had with the *Messenger*, Poe threw himself into hard work—proofreading, performing editorial duties, and writing harsh critical reviews on a myriad of subjects.

In *Burton's*, he also published two of his most famous tales, "The Fall of the House of Usher" and "William Wilson." His first volume of short stories, *Tales of the Grotesque and Arabesque*, a work of five hundred pages, was printed in two volumes in December 1839. By this time, Poe's reputation was growing. Dozens of periodicals praised his magazine writing as "unusually excellent," called his stories "some of the most popular tales of American origin," and claimed that his *Tales* placed him "in the foremost rank of American writers" (154–155). After working for Burton for a year, the two men parted company on bad terms, Burton accusing Poe of failing in his duties because of drunkenness, a charge Poe denied, and Poe alleging that Burton was a scoundrel (157–158).

Immediately Poe tried to set up his own literary journal, *Penn Magazine*. Having his own magazine was a career-long ambition because Poe realized "that he would not succeed as a magazinist unless he controlled the product of his labor" (Weiner, 11). Furthermore, he recognized that the magazine "became the vehicle for serious, important literature" (Hayes, 115). Poe hoped to

WHILE POE WAS WORKING AT *BURTON'S*, HE PUBLISHED HIS OWN STORIES IN THE MAGAZINE, INCLUDING "THE FALL OF THE HOUSE OF USHER."

begin publication in January 1841, but, because of his illness and a financial panic, the magazine had to be indefinitely postponed and was never published.

That spring, Poe took a job as editor of *Graham's*, the former *Burton's Gentlemen's Magazine*, which was now under the ownership of George Rex Graham, a man who paid Poe eight hundred dollars a year (worth about $16,000 in 2008). As editor, Poe once again wrote critical reviews of works and often harshly criticized other American writers such as Henry Wadsworth Longfellow and William Cullen Bryant. However, one writer he thoroughly praised was Nathaniel Hawthorne, whose *Twice-Told Tales* Poe greatly admired. Poe remained busy writing his own short stories, and in April 1841 he published "The Murders in the Rue Morgue." This was the first modern detective story, or, as Poe called it, tale of "ratiocination," which means logical reasoning. Under Poe's leadership, *Graham's* grew at a surprising rate, from 5,500 subscribers in 1841 to over 40,000 in early 1842 (Silverman, *Edgar A. Poe*, 174).

Poe's dream of having his own literary journal stayed with him, and, for a while, he and Graham planned to go into partnership to produce this work, which Poe now planned to name *Stylus*. But Graham lost interest, and Poe grew tired of slaving on *Graham's*. In April 1842, he left the magazine on good terms with Graham, who later wrote of Poe: "he was always the same polished gentleman—the quiet, unobtrusive, thoughtful scholar—the devoted husband—frugal in his personal expenses—punctual and unwearied in his industry—*and the soul of honor*, in all his transactions" (quoted in A. H. Quinn, 342). Graham also remarked on his devotion to his family: "I shall never forget how solicitous of the happiness of his wife and mother-in-law he was. . . . Except for their happiness—and the natural ambition of having a magazine of his own—I never heard him deplore the want of wealth. The truth is, he cared little for money. . . . What he received from me in regular monthly instalments [sic], went directly into the hands of his mother-in-law for family comforts" (343).

Part of Poe's unhappiness at *Graham's* stemmed from something that had nothing to do with work. In January, Virginia had begun bleeding from her mouth while she was singing. Although Poe denied the severity of her disease, calling it a "ruptured blood vessel" caused by a singing accident (*Letters*, Vol. 1, 191), Virginia was really suffering from tuberculosis. Her struggle with death probably inspired two stories: "Life in Death" and "The Mask of the Red Death" (later spelled "Masque").

With Virginia's illness, Poe also became sick and often drank to relieve his anxieties. Years later Poe explained his situation: "Her life was despaired of. I took leave of her forever & underwent all the agonies of her death." These agonies were repeated multiple times. "She recovered partially and I again hoped. At the end of a year the vessel broke again—I went through precisely the same scene. Again in about a year afterward. Then again again again & even once again at varying intervals." Each time she became worse, he suffered terribly. "I became insane, with long intervals of horrible sanity. During these fits of absolute unconsciousness, I drank." Although his enemies said that drinking drove him to insanity, Poe says that it was insanity that drove him to drinking because of "the horrible never-ending oscillation between hope & despair which I could *not* longer have endured without the total loss of reason" (*Letters*, Vol. 2, 356). Making things worse was Poe's unusual sensitivity to alcohol; Muddy related that after drinking one or two glasses of wine "he was not responsible for either his words, or actions" (quoted in Silverman, *Edgar A. Poe*, 184). By May of 1843, his drinking habit was well-known in Philadelphia.

Too poor to even file bankruptcy papers, Poe decided to try to get a government post, hoping to work at a custom house as Hawthorne had done, but he was unable to land a position. His dreams of having his own magazine remained alive, but his efforts to secure a partner failed. What little money Poe made in the twenty months after leaving *Graham's* was obtained through lecturing and writing. In 1843 and 1844, he gave several two-hour lectures on poetry in America. Like his mother, Poe was an accomplished performer. In reviews, he was called a "correct and graceful reader." He was commended for his "command of language and strength of voice,"and his lec-

POE LOVED LIVING IN PHILADELPHIA, BUT HIS INABILITY TO FIND A JOB FINALLY FORCED HIM TO MOVE TO NEW YORK.

ture was called "an eloquent production eloquently delivered" (quoted in Silverman, *Edgar A. Poe*, 218). He also made some money by publishing "The Pit and the Pendulum," "The Tell-Tale Heart," "The Black Cat," "The Mystery of Marie Rogêt," and "The Gold-Bug," for which he won one hundred dollars, first prize in a story contest. All these tales are still well-known.

During the six years Poe lived in Philadelphia, he met many writers, actors, and journalists. He had known success, and his fame as a writer was spreading. According to Arthur Hobson Quinn, "he was even happy, and when he left it, it is not too much to say that he left happiness behind him" (404). However, with no steady income, Poe had to try to get a job someplace, and nothing was available in Philadelphia.

New York Once Again: 1844-1847

In April 1844, Poe and Virginia, and later Muddy, returned to New York and, after boarding in the city for a short time, lived on a beautiful farm about five miles out of the city. Poe worked as a correspondent for various newspapers until he found permanent work with the New York *Mirror*, earning fifteen dollars a week. His new employer, Nathaniel Parker Willis, found him a model employee—"a quiet, patient, industrious, and most gentlemanly person, commanding the utmost respect and good feeling by his unvarying deportment and ability" (quoted in A. H. Quinn, 434). Poe continued to write stories, including "The Purloined Letter," which he felt was "perhaps, the best of my tales of ratiocination" (*Letters*, Vol. 1, 258).

In January 1845, Poe became a celebrity with the publication of "The Raven," a poem that Poe must have written in a time of despair when he thought Virginia was dying. The *New World* reported that "Everybody reads the Poem and praises it, . . . justly we think, for it seems to us full of originality and power" (quoted in Silverman,

Edgar A. Poe, 237). In February, *Graham's Magazine* published a biography of Poe written by the American author James Russell Lowell. Lowell praised Poe as a creative writer who has "two of the prime qualities of genius—a faculty of vigorous yet minute analysis, and a wonderful fecundity of imagination" (12). Lowell went on to say that as a literary critic, Poe was "the most discriminate, philosophical, and fearless critic upon imaginative works who has written in America" (6).

Early in 1845, Poe's family moved from the farm back to the city, where Poe took a new job with better opportunities, becoming an editor for the *Broadway Journal* with a share of the possible profits. Once again, he toiled on a magazine, "working 14 or 15 hours a day" (*Letters*, Vol. 1, 286), but made little money. As he had done in the *Mirror*, Poe continued to attack other writers and, thus, alienated a number of literary men and women. As an editor, however, Poe was, once again, superb.

Always sociable, Poe, and sometimes Virginia, attended parties held by the New York literary societies. One hostess, Anne Charlotte Lynch, described him as an ideal guest, elegantly dressed and having "always the bearing and manners of a gentleman, . . . interesting in conversation, but not monopolizing; polite and engaging. . . . quiet and unaffected, unpretentious, in his manner" (quoted in Silverman, *Edgar Allan Poe*, 279). In 1845, Poe became good friends with the poet, Frances (Fanny) Osgood, an intelligent woman who deeply cared for him. Osgood was also a friend of Poe's family, and Virginia, now exceedingly sick and concerned about her husband's well-being after she died, encouraged their friendship, feeling that Osgood's good influence helped Poe stay away from alcohol. However, the New York literary crowds frowned on their friendship—in part because of the jealousy of other women who wished to flirt with Poe—and soon banned Poe from the literary circles.

THOUGH POE'S WIFE LOOKED KINDLY ON HIS FRIENDSHIP WITH THE
POET FRANCES OSGOOD (ABOVE), OTHERS IN HIS LITERARY CIRCLE
WERE JEALOUS.

In October, Poe's elusive dream of owning his own magazine came true when he became a partner and sole publisher and manager of the floundering *Broadway Journal*. But, despite his herculean efforts, Poe, with no capital, could not keep the magazine going, and it died with its January 3, 1846, issue.

To try to improve Virginia's health, Poe moved his family out of New York to a modest cottage in the village of Fordham (now part of the Bronx, a New York City borough), thirteen miles from the city. As Virginia lay dying of tuberculosis, Poe also suffered from an undiagnosed disease, so sick he often was unable to get out of bed, causing people to openly speculate that he had lost his sanity. In spite of the Poes' poverty and illness, the sparsely furnished Fordham cottage, like all of the family's residences, had "an air of taste and gentility that must have been lent to it by the presence of its inmates. So neat, so poor, so unfurnished, and yet so charming a dwelling I never saw" (Mary Gove Nichols, quoted in A. H. Quinn, 508–509).

Here the three lived together with great love and respect for one another. Poe lovingly called Muddy "our Mother," and he was always "soft, concerned, nearly reverential" with Virginia (Silverman, *Edgar A. Poe*, 303). Poe's letter reveals his love and gentleness as he addresses Virginia as "my Dear Heart," and "my little darling wife," and credited her with being "my *greatest* and *only* stimulus now, to battle with this uncongenial, unsatisfactory and ungrateful life" (*Letters*, Vol. 2, 318).

When the move did not help Virginia recover, Poe became more and more anxious, letting out his frustrations in a literary warfare that he began by writing sketches of writers called "The Literati of New York City" that were published in Philadelphia's *Godey's Lady's Book*. As he had throughout his career as a literary critic, he offered some words of praise for other writers but, most of the time, many words of condemnation. Problems erupted when he painted Thomas Dunn English as an uneducated fool who ruined his magazine because of his ignorance of grammar. English responded by accusing Poe of forgery and of being "an assassin in morals" (quoted in A. H. Quinn, 504), publishing his attack in the *Mirror*, which was no longer owned by Poe's friend Willis. Poe filed a libel suit against the new owners of the magazine and, after a number of months, was awarded "$225.06 in damages, and court costs of $101.42" (Silverman, *Edgar A. Poe*, 328).

In spite of troubles, Poe wrote a wonderful tale, "The Cask of Amontillado," which was published in November 1846.

By November, Virginia had no hope of living. Guests were filled with sympathy when they saw the poverty in the Poe household as Virginia lay dying "in her neat, scanty room, lying on a straw mattress with snow-white sheets, often covered, as the cold of winter approached, with Poe's old military cloak, shivering in the hectic fever of consumption" (Silverman, *Edgar A. Poe*, 323). With the financial help of Willis and the physical aid of a widow, Marie Louise (Loui) Shew, the family survived The day before her death, Virginia, still sweet and loving, joined Poe's and Shew's hands and said, "Mary, be a friend to Eddie, and don't forsake him; he always loved you—didn't you, Eddie?'" (quoted on 326). The next day, January 30, 1847, after an agonizing night, Virginia Poe was dead at age twenty-five. She was buried on February 2. Many years later, her body was transferred to Baltimore where it now lies next to her husband.

Both Poe and Muddy were devastated by Virginia's death. In great distress, Poe would sometimes sneak out of his house late on the winter nights to visit her grave, wearing only his stockings so he would not wake Muddy. After the long strain of watching his beloved wife die, Poe collapsed. Shew, who had medical training, found that his heart beat irregularly and concluded that he suffered from a brain lesion made worse by a fever caused by "actual want and hunger, and cold having been borne by this heroic husband in order to supply food, medicine, and comforts to his dying wife" (quoted in A. H. Quinn, 528).

By summer 1847, Poe was better physically, mentally, and financially, as a result of his successful lawsuit. He was able to write one of his finest poems, "Ulalume," a compelling work about a man's human passions for a living woman and the spiritual love he continues to feel for the memory of dead Ulalume.

Last Years: 1848-1849

His most ambitious work of 1848 was the prose poem *Eureka*, which he started in 1847 and first read in New York City. The work is Poe's analysis of the fundamental nature of the universe and the purpose of life and death as part of a cosmic plan. When it was published in the summer of 1848, some reviewers found it a magnificent scientific work that would bring "unfailing lustre [sic] upon the American name" because it showed "a degree of logical acumen which has certainly not been equalled [sic] since the days of Sir Isaac Newton," but others attacked it for its pantheism, which they considered "blasphemy" (quoted in Silverman, *Edgar A. Poe*, 341–342).

Convinced that he needed to find a loving woman who would stabilize him as Virginia had done, Poe, age thirty-nine, became involved with several female friends in 1848 after Loui Shew distanced herself from him because she was offended by the religious views Poe expressed in *Eureka*. One was poet Sarah Helen Whitman, a forty-five-year-old widow who lived in Providence, Rhode Island. When Helen seemed to break off their romance in November, Poe, extremely upset, tried to commit suicide by taking an ounce of laudanum,

AFTER VIRGINIA'S DEATH, POE BECAME ENGAGED TO POET SARAH HELEN WHITMAN, BUT SHE BROKE THE ENGAGEMENT BECAUSE HER MOTHER WAS UNHAPPY ABOUT IT.

a type of opium that was a common cure for headaches. Because he unintentionally overdosed, he vomited some of it up, and his life was saved. Helen and Poe then became briefly engaged, but she broke off the engagement, mainly because her mother objected. Poe and Helen seemed to have true affection but not passionate love for each other. Poe wrote his second poem titled "To Helen" to her and published it in 1848. In 1850, Helen seemed sad that she had not married Poe, writing, he was "one whose sweet and gracious nature had endeared him to me beyond expression, and whose rare and peculiar intellect had given a new charm to my life" (Thomas and Jackson, 795).

The woman Poe passionately loved was from Lowell, Massachusetts: Nancy Locke Heywood Richmond, whom he called "Annie." She was the twenty-eight-year-old wife of a wealthy manufacturer, and the mother of a small child. Although she had no intention of breaking up her family and always acted with self-respect, Poe urged Annie to come and live near Muddy and him. Annie became Poe's confidante and was devoted to him, finding him *unlike* any other person," "incomparable," "not to be measured by any ordinary standard" (Thomas and Jackson, 741).

While courting Helen and Annie in 1848, Poe wrote little, but he did compose his best critical essay on poetry, "The Poetic Principle," which he gave as a lecture the following year in both Richmond and Norfolk, Virginia. In 1849 he wrote some of his best poetry. The first poems published that year were autobiographical. "To My Mother" praises Muddy, while both "Landor's Cottage" and "For Annie" celebrate Annie Richmond. Although many women thought "Annabel Lee" was written for them, Silverman concludes that "Annabel Lee represents all of the women he loved and lost" (*Edgar A. Poe*, 402). He wrote two other poems that year: "Eldorado" and "The Bells."

Spring 1849 was another time of illness for Poe, who lay at the Fordham cottage so sick that Muddy "thought he would *die* several times" (*Letters*, Vol. 2, 437–438). However, his spirits were lifted in April when he received a letter from Edward Horton Norton Patterson, a young writer and editor who wanted to hire Poe to be editor of a magazine in Illinois. At long last, Poe's dream of the *Stylus* seemed to be a possibility. To raise money for this project, Poe needed to get subscribers, and he decided to travel to Richmond for this purpose and then go to St. Louis to meet Patterson.

On June 30, he left for Virginia, stopping in Philadelphia, where there was a cholera epidemic. Poe became sick and stayed some days, writing to Muddy, "My *dear, dear* Mother,—I have been *so* ill—have had the cholera, or spasms quite as bad, and can now hardly hold the pen" (*Letters*, Vol. 2, 452). To fight the disease, Poe took calomel, a type of mercury, which made him sicker, "worse than death" (*Letters*, Vol. 2, 457). Although Silverman does not think that Poe had cholera, Poe was very sick and suffered from hallucinations, thinking some men were trying to kill him. Poe later wrote to Muddy that his hallucinations arose "from an attack which I had never before experienced—an attack of *mania-à-potu*," delirium tremens caused by drinking (*Letters*, Vol. 2, 455). After being cared for by friends, Poe was well enough to travel to Richmond and arrived on July 14.

Back in his boyhood hometown, Poe seems to have taken a new interest in life. He lectured on "The Poetic Principle," which received excellent reviews; critics described the lecture as "full of strong, manly sense," and called it "one of the richest intellectual treats we have ever had the good fortune to hear" (quoted in Silverman, *Edgar A. Poe*, 425). Poe also decided to totally abstain from alcohol, and he joined the Sons of Temperance, a move he probably made because he had become so sick after drinking heavily that the doctors feared he would die. In addition, Poe renewed his childhood romance with Elmira Royster Shelton, now a wealthy widow. Expecting to marry Elmira soon, Poe left for New York to move Muddy to Richmond to live with them. The night before he left, he called on Elmira, who found him so sick with a fever that she did not think he could travel. That same evening, he went to see Dr. John Carter. After a late supper, he left Richmond on a steamer headed for Baltimore on the morning of September 27.

Last Days: September 27–October 3, 1849

There is no trustworthy evidence of what happened to Poe during the next seven days, from the time he left for Baltimore on September 27 to October 3 when he was found in a semiconscious state outside Gunner's Hall, a tavern in Baltimore that served as a polling place during elections. The man who found him, Joseph Walker, sent for Dr. Joseph Evans Snodgrass, describing Poe as "rather the worse for wear" and "in great distress" (quoted in Silverman, *Edgar A. Poe*, 433). Finding Poe in an armchair dressed in "neither vest nor tie, his dingy trousers fit badly, his shirt was crumpled, his cheap hat soiled" (434), a manner of dress unheard of for the fastidious Poe, Snodgrass assumed that Poe was drunk and had been robbed of his own clothes.

Snodgrass and Henry Herring, Poe's uncle by marriage, sent Poe, now "insensible, muttering" (Thomas and Jackson, 844–845), to the hospital at Washington Medical College that afternoon. His attending physician, John J. Moran, reported that he was unconscious until the next afternoon, when his limbs began trembling and he developed "a busy, but not violent or active delirium" (quoted in Silverman, *Edgar A. Poe*, 434). Pale and drenched in sweat, Poe talked unceasingly, addressing "spectral and imaginary objects on the walls" (434). Although Moran questioned him about his condition, Poe's answers were incoherent. His cousin, Neilson Poe, came to visit, but he was not admitted because Poe was in too excitable a condition. When Neilson returned the next day with clean linen, he was told that his cousin had improved. But soon, Moran said that Poe was violently delirious, raving for more than a day, repeatedly calling out the name "Reynolds." At 3:00 a.m. on Sunday, October 7, he rested briefly, and then, according to Moran, "quietly moving his head, he said 'Lord help my poor Soul' and expired!" (quoted on 435).

The cause of Poe's death is unclear. Because Poe was well known for his drinking binges, particularly during Virginia's illness, many people think that he became intoxicated, fell sick, and died. Snodgrass was convinced that Poe's death was caused by alcohol, as was Poe's friend, John P. Kennedy, who recorded in his diary that Poe died of "debauch" after falling "in with some companion here who seduced him to the bottle" (quoted in C. H. Bonner, 194). But Moran positively stated that Poe was not drunk, and furthermore, this theory does not explain why he was wearing cheap clothing that did not belong to him.

Another explanation for Poe's death is that he died from "congestion of the brain" or "cerebral inflammation" (Silverman, *Edgar A. Poe*, 435). This goes along with the diagnosis made by one of Moran's senior physicians that Poe died of encephalitis, which he defined as an inflammation of the brain caused by exposure (436). This explanation of exposure, if not the name of the disease, seems plausible because Poe, clothed in lightweight garments, was found outdoors during very cold weather. Also, it is consistent with Elmira Shelton's statement that he had a fever when he left Richmond. Other diseases have also been suggested as possible causes of Poe's death, including stroke, enzyme disorder, toxic blood disorder, tuberculosis, epilepsy, diabetes, meningitis, hypoglycemia, brain hemorrhage, and rabies. Dying from some sort of disease seems logical because Poe had been very sick in the years before his death, diagnosed as suffering from brain lesions, brain fever, and a weak heart.

Some people suggest that Poe died because he was the victim of voting fraud called "cooping," an illegal but common election-day practice in Baltimore. According to this theory, unscrupulous men from a political party kidnapped Poe, plied him with liquor, beat him to ensure his obedience, forced him to wear someone else's clothes so he would not be recognized, hauled him from one polling site to another to vote for their favorites under different identities, and left him to die (Miller, 49). This theory, although it cannot be proven, has some credibility because Poe was found on election day near a tavern that also served as a place for voting. Furthermore, he was wearing someone else's clothes.

On either October 8 (Silverman, *Edgar A. Poe*, 436) or October 9 (Ingram, 428; A. H. Quinn, 642), a very small funeral was conducted by the Reverend William T. D. Clemm, one of Virginia's cousins, at Westminster Presbyterian graveyard. Only four people attended: Poe's relatives, Neilsen Poe and Henry Herring; Poe's friend, Joseph Snodgrass; and Poe's former classmate, Z. Collins Lee. His body was buried close to his grandfather near the center of the graveyard.

Muddy did not know about his death until she read about it in a New York newspaper on October 9 (Silverman, 437). In the following years, she lived off the generosity of Poe's friends, moving from one home to another, until 1863, when she became a charity case at the Church Home in Baltimore. It had once been the hospital of Washington Medical College, the place Poe died. Muddy died there on February 16, 1871; she was eighty-one years old.

ONLY FOUR PEOPLE ATTENDED POE'S FUNERAL, BUT IN THE YEARS SINCE HIS DEATH, MILLIONS OF FANS OF HIS WRITING HAVE KEPT HIS FAME ALIVE.

Poe's sister, Rosalie, continued to live "in Richmond with the MacKensies until after the Civil War, which impoverished and broke up the family" (Silverman, *Edgar A. Poe*, 441). Homeless and friendless, she tried to earn money by selling pictures of her famous brother. In 1874, when she was sixty-four, Rosalie was admitted to Epiphany Church Home, a charity shelter in Washington, D.C. She died there on July 21, 1874.

In 1875, Poe's coffin was moved to a prominent position in the southwestern corner of the cemetery. Beside him are buried Virginia and Muddy.

Ruined Reputation

Immediately after his death, Poe was slandered by Rufus Wilmot Griswold, who effectively destroyed Poe's reputation. Griswold was a magazine editor from Philadelphia whom Poe met in May 1841 while working at *Graham's*. Griswold paid Poe to review an anthology he had written and was furious when Poe did not praise his work to his expectations. In 1843 and 1844, when Poe turned to lecturing, according to Silverman, he lampooned Griswold as a "tasteless New Englander, unashamed puffer, and follower of the herd" (*Edgar A. Poe*, 218). Griswold responded by bad-mouthing Poe to other writers. Although years later Poe thought the two of them had become friends—and unfortunately asked Griswold to serve as his literary executor if he died—Griswold still hated Poe. With Poe's sudden death in 1849, Griswold immediately set out to ruin his reputation.

He started by writing a malicious obituary on October 9, which he anonymously signed as "Ludwig." His malevolent picture of Poe began in his opening paragraph: "Edgar Allan Poe is dead. He died in Baltimore the day before yesterday. This announcement will startle many *but few will be grieved by it*. The poet was well known personally or by reputation, in all this country; he had

RUFUS GRISWOLD WOULD BE UNKNOWN TODAY IF HE HAD NOT
WRITTEN A BIOGRAPHY OF POE SO VICIOUS THAT IT DAMAGED HIS
REPUTATION FOR CENTURIES, PERHAPS FOR ALL TIME.

readers in England, and in several of the states of Continental Europe; *but he had few or no friends*; and the regrets for his death will be suggested principally by the consideration that in him literary art lost one of its most brilliant, but erratic, stars" (28).

Although many friends and writers renounced the claims made by "Ludwig," Griswold's obituary was widely printed and, therefore, was deemed the true story of Poe. Furthermore, as Poe's literary executor, every time he published Poe's works, Griswold introduced them with a "Memoir" of Poe in which he elaborated the false claims made in the obituary and even altered Poe's letters to make him seem malicious to his friends. Since Griswold had control of Poe's works, he was able to publish and republish his memoir. Griswold did such a convincing job of describing Poe as a drunkard, a debtor, a criminal, a drug addict, and an immoral person who suffered from insanity that Poe's reputation is still marred 160 years after his death.

Griswold's description of Poe contradicts the descriptions of those who knew him. Although Poe was a harsh literary critic, he was loving and generous to acquaintances and family members. Person after person has remarked on his gentlemanly qualities, his total devotion to Virginia and Muddy, his kindnesses to others, his industrious work habits, and his high, uncompromising standards of excellence.

Two of Griswold's charges had some truth. First, Poe did have a drinking problem, but his main trouble was a low tolerance for alcohol, not overindulgence. Second, Poe often begged for and borrowed money because he was extremely poor, but he never committed fraud or any other criminal act. Griswold's claim that Poe was a drug addict is simply untrue; even English, whom Poe had successfully sued for libel a few years earlier, adamantly discredited this allegation, calling it "baseless slander" (quoted in A. H. Quinn, 350). Poe's ignorance regarding how much laudanum to take when he wanted to commit suicide attests to his lack of experience with drugs. The Poe legend established by Griswold is, thus, unfounded, unsupported, and false.

Edgar Allan Poe was a gifted writer; a brilliant thinker; an industrious and honorable worker; a warm and kind friend; a courteous host; a self-sacrificing, devoted husband and son-in-law; a chivalrous gentleman of utter refinement; and an artist of highest standards. He unwisely drank, sometimes to be sociable but often to relieve his melancholy and depression caused by the early deaths of loved ones, poverty, sickness, and lack of appreciation for his talents. Robert Bloch's words, written more than three decades ago, remain true today: "The name and fame of Edgar Allan Poe are secure at last. But it is the public Poe whose work we praise, while our debt to the real man must now and forever remain unpaid—the sad and lonely man who, out of mortal misery, created immortal mystery" (7).

THE BRITISH CAPTURED THE CITY OF WASHINGTON, D.C., IN 1814. THAT MIGHT HAVE RESULTED IN THE END OF THE UNITED STATES, IF THE AMERICAN SOLDIERS HADN'T STAVED OFF THE BRITISH IN BALTIMORE, IN A BATTLE IN WHICH POE'S GRANDFATHER PLAYED A PART.

evermore." Suddenly, he hears a tapping at his chamber d
though filled with fear, he tells himself that some vis
s come and opens the door. When no one appears, he imag
at Lenore may have knocked and whispers her name, hea
ly an echo murmuring back. Returning to his chamber
ce again hears the tapping, this time louder. Assuming
e wind rattling his door, he opens a shutter, and a sta
ven steps into his chamber and perches on the bust of Pa
ove his chamber door. When he asks its name, the r
plies, "Nevermore." The lonely poet thinks that the r

Chapter 2

Poe's Times

WHEN POE WAS BORN IN 1809, the young United States was experiencing tensions with England, which was interfering with American shipping. In 1812, shortly after Edgar became a ward of the Allans, the War of 1812 began. Things became desperate for America in 1814 when the British captured Washington, D.C., and burned the Capitol. But when they tried to overthrow Baltimore a few weeks later, they were met with a stiff defense, organized by patriotic men, including Poe's grandfather. It was the battle in Baltimore, in which the British were repelled, that inspired American lawyer Francis Scott Key to write the "Star-Spangled Banner."

After peace was restored in 1814, John Allan and his partner decided to expand their business by opening an office in London. In 1815, Allan moved his family, including six-year-old Edgar, to England where his business prospered. Throughout America, the economy flourished, aided by economic measures that were put in place to protect American manufacturers and farmers from foreign competitors. Optimistic people pressed westward in search of more opportunities, new states were added to the union, and two new territories were acquired. In 1818, Britain gave America the Red River basin, an area north of the Louisiana territory, and the following year, Spain ceded Florida to the United States. The prosperous years the Allans spent in England, 1815 to 1820, have been called the Era of Good Feeling because of the hopefulness, peace, and unity found in America.

When the Allans and eleven-year-old Edgar Poe returned to Virginia in 1820 after Allan's London business failed, the issue of slavery was causing much divisiveness between Northerners and Southerners. This growing problem was publicly recognized by Congress, which passed the Missouri Compromise that year, agreeing to admit one free state, Maine, at the same time as it admitted one slave state, Missouri. For the first time, Congress was forced to both debate "the morality of slavery" and address "the diverging interests of free and slave states" (Kennedy, 21).

With the slavery question answered for a time, Poe and his fellow Americans anticipated a bright future. The nation continued to move further westward in the 1820s, a development that was aided by President James Monroe's 1822 Monroe Doctrine, a policy that warned European countries not to interfere with any nation in the Americas. New forms of transportation also helped in the western expansion. Many canals were built, making it easier for people to move west and for goods to move east. The most important, the Erie Canal, which joins the Hudson River in New York to the Great Lakes, opened in 1825. Railroads were also constructed. When Poe was a small child, there were no railroads, but by the time he died, there were ten thousand miles of track (Whalen, "American Publishing Industry," 65). Freed from foreign entanglements and aided by better means of transportation, brave pioneers searched for a better life in unsettled American land.

In the eastern part of the country, education became greatly valued. New colleges were formed, and young men were encouraged to enroll. One new school was the University of Virginia, which Poe attended in 1826.

While most Americans continued to enjoy prosperity in the late 1820s, Poe, cast out by John Allan in 1827, was trying to survive. He was only nineteen when Andrew Jackson, an uneducated Democrat from Tennessee, was elected president in 1828, winning a contest that "transformed presidential elections forever by introducing national political tactics, fierce partisanship, and the appeal to a popular electorate through campaign spending" (Kennedy, 26). He remained in office for eight years. With a common man in national politics, the country became more democratic. According to Terence Whalen, "his presidency would have offered Poe a formula for success (appeal to the masses) and an easy polemical target (the wealthy gentleman)" ("American Publishing Industry," 65).

As Poe struggled to make a living in the army, at West Point, and as a writer, other citizens were also experiencing hard times. Many pioneers, embracing the doctrine of manifest destiny, the idea that the United States should control the entire North American continent, continued to push westward. As a result, the United States was involved in conflicts with American Indians, Mexico, and Great Britain, which owned huge areas of land. In 1830, Jackson supported the Removal Bill that authorized the evacuation of eastern Indian tribes to lands west of the Mississippi. When the Cherokees of Georgia, who first resisted the move, were evicted from their land and forced to move west, thousands died on a route that has become known as the Trail of Tears.

Trouble with Mexico began in 1835 when Americans in Texas revolted against Mexico and declared Texas a sovereign nation. In 1844, Texas was annexed by the United States. That same year, Britain, not feeling it was worth the trouble to keep the Oregon Territory, ceded it to the United States. More trouble with Mexico developed in the following years, resulting in the Mexican War, which was fought from 1846 to 1848. With its defeat, Mexico gave more land to the United States—525,000 square miles stretching from the Rio Grande west to the Pacific and north to the Oregon Territory. Thus, by the time of Poe's death in 1849, the United States owned almost all of the lands that make up present-day America,

THE TRAIL OF TEARS HAS BECOME A SYMBOL OF THE INJUSTICE WITH WHICH AMERICAN INDIANS WERE SERVED BY THE U.S. GOVERNMENT IN THE NINETEENTH CENTURY.

except southern Arizona and New Mexico (purchased from Mexico in 1853), Alaska (purchased from Russia in 1867), and Hawaii (annexed in 1898). The nation had grown from seventeen states in 1809 to thirty in 1849, and extended from Maine to Florida, and from Massachusetts to Texas.

At the same time that Americans were moving west, large cities were developing, particularly on the eastern seaboard. New York City grew quickly, more than doubling its population between 1820 and 1840 from 123,000 to 310,000. Other cities, including Boston, Philadelphia, New Orleans, and Cincinnati, also had populations of over 100,000 (Kennedy, 33). During Poe's lifetime, the nation's population more than tripled, growing from about 7 million to 23 million (Blair, et. al, 78, 139). With the rise of huge cities, a new reading public was established, and periodicals began flourishing in the 1830s. At the same time, better printing technology and paper production processes were developed, all of which led to "a periodical trade that expanded rapidly and produced new opportunities for aspiring writers, editors, and publishers. Newspapers, magazines, and reviews, together with publishing houses, bookstores, and itinerant booksellers, created the framework for an emerging American mass culture" (Kennedy, 23). This was a major development for Poe, both as a writer and an editor of a number of magazines.

As a literary editor, one of the topics Poe had to deal with was the continuing issue of slavery, the greatest conflict of Poe's lifetime. Although Poe, trying to keep the support of both northerners and southerners for his magazines, did not take sides, the government had to confront the problem. Officials tried many compromises, but tensions continued to build. Territories were admitted to the United States based on whether they would be slave or free states. Thus, the westward movement widened the gulf between abolitionists and slave owners.

While the nation expanded and flourished, Americans, proud of their country, wanted uniquely American literature. As a result, literature flourished even though almost all of the literary giants struggled financially and worked day jobs to support themselves. A number of authors helped form the American Renaissance, writing in three main literary forms: essay, fiction, and poetry. Only Poe was recognized as a leader in all three genres. Other leading essayists included James Russell Lowell, Oliver Wendell Holmes, Henry David Thoreau, and Ralph Waldo Emerson. In fiction, two early writers, Washington Irving and James Fenimore Cooper, were looked upon as literary icons. Three younger men later became famous— Poe and Nathaniel Hawthorne as short story writers, and Hawthorne and Herman Melville as novelists. American poets were also thriving, including Henry Wadsworth Longfellow (whom Poe bitterly attacked as an overrated writer), Holmes, Lowell, Emerson, Thoreau, and Poe. Scholar Walter Blair declares that the "American Renaissance was one of the richest periods in our literary history, not only in its concepts and perceptions but also in its embodiments of them" (137). Not only were many literary pieces produced during Poe's lifetime, but many of them were also recognized as serious works of art.

In the year of Poe's death, 1849, the gold rush had begun, and hordes of opportunists rushed to California to try to get rich. Despite the optimism, tensions continued to grow between the North and South, as the issue of slavery divided the Union. A little more than a decade after Poe's death, the Civil War broke out.

Chapter 3

Poe's Tales

DURING HIS LIFETIME, Poe was well-known as a writer of short stories, publishing sixty-eight tales. He is most famous for two kinds of stories: Gothic tales of horror that explore the dark side of human life, including death, murder, violence, ghosts, and haunted landscapes, and the modern detective stories, which he called "tales of ratiocination," a new form he developed.

Unlike many writers, Poe felt that the short story, not the novel, was the best form of fiction since it is "a highly crafted work of art destined to withstand the ages" (Hayes, 73). Because readers are able to take in a tale at one sitting with no interruptions, they can then experience "the unity of effect or impression" which makes a psychological impact on them by producing "high excitement" and "an exaltation of the soul" (Poe, *The Complete Tales and Poems*, 949). To achieve one effect, the writer needs to carefully structure the story so there is "no word written, of which the tendency, direct or indirect, is not to the one pre-established design" (950).

Many of Poe's tales have become classics. Although "The Black Cat," "Ligeia," *The Narrative of Arthur Gordon Pym*, "William Wilson," and "MS. Found in a Bottle" are well-known and greatly admired, this chapter will only focus on those tales most frequently studied by high school students: "The Cask of Amontillado," "The Fall of the House of Usher," "The Masque of the Red Death," "The Murders in the Rue Morgue," "The Pit and the Pendulum," "The Purloined Letter," and "The Tell-Tale Heart."

This 1935 illustration by Arthur Rackham shows Fortunato and Montresor in "The Cask of Amontillado."

"The Cask of Amontillado" (1846)

Montresor is the narrator of this chilling tale of revenge and murder. Stating that he has been insulted by his fellow townsman, Fortunato, he plots perfect revenge by punishing his victim with impunity while letting him know who has done it. One night during a carnival, Montresor meets Fortunato and tells him that he has purchased expensive Amontillado wine but needs an expert's opinion on whether it is truly Amontillado. He entices Fortunato, who is proud of his knowledge of wine, to go with him into the Montresor catacombs to examine the wine. As they travel deeper and deeper into the vaults, Montresor, pretending to be concerned about Fortunato's health, which is aggravated by the dampness, offers to get Fortunato's rival, Luchesi, to come in Fortunato's place, causing Fortunato to become more eager to continue. At one point, Fortunato tells Montresor that he has forgotten the Montresor family coat of arms and motto. Later, he makes an unusual hand gesture that Montresor does not recognize as a secret sign of the Masons. At the end of the catacombs, the men enter a small niche where Montresor chains Fortunato and begins enclosing him in a brick wall. No one has disturbed Fortunato's bones since he was buried.

When Montresor tells this story fifty years later, he is an old man. He is talking to someone who, he says, knows "so well the nature of my soul" (666), possibly a priest or a confidant. Although some readers think that Montresor is insane because he is a murderer, this story is not the rantings of a madman. In fact, what makes it so chilling is the fear that Montresor is sane—that a rational man would gloat about a cold-blooded murder he committed, serving as judge, juror, and executioner of a fellow citizen who is in the act of doing him a favor.

One reason readers think Montresor is insane is that they feel he has no real motive for killing Fortunato because he does not directly state the nature of Fortunato's insult. However, as Elena V. Baraban argues, Montresor may be punishing Fortunato for arrogantly thinking he is socially superior. She points out that Montresor differentiates between "injuries," which "presuppose rivalry of socially equal enemies," and "insult," which "involves contempt: that is, threatening the other as a socially inferior person" (50).

As seen twice in the story, Fortunato does insult Montresor. First, he forgets the Montresor family coat of arms and motto, well-known details of prominent families, which other leading families would not forget. G. R. Thompson stresses the magnitude of this blunder, writing that Fortunato acts "unforgivably" by failing to remember them (*Selected Writings*, 418n6). Second, Fortunato implies that Montresor lacks the social prominence to be a part of the elite brotherhood of freemasons, mocking Montresor for saying that he is a Mason: "You? Impossible! A mason?" (669).

These are degrading statements to make to another nobleman, a man wealthy enough to have a number of servants, a large palazzo, expensive Amontillado, and huge wine vaults. In spite of Fortunato's greater social status, the Montresor family was once as powerful, as implied by the narrator's statements, "You are rich, respected, admired, beloved; you are happy, as once I was. You are a man to be missed" (668). Montresor may even have "a better aristocratic lineage than Fortunato" (Baraban, 51), as seen by the extensive family catacombs, a sign that they "were a great and numerous family" (669).

Although financially and socially inferior at the time of the story, Montresor rightly regards himself as intellectually superior to Fortunato. A brilliant man who understands human nature, Montresor knows how to manipulate people by using reverse psychology. He tricks his servants into leaving the house by giving them strict orders to stay home while he is gone, understanding that such "orders were sufficient . . . to insure their immediate disappearance . . . as soon as [his] back was turned" (668). He is also able to control Fortunato. He astutely figures out that he can use Fortunato's pride as a wine connoisseur to lure him to his crypt, and then he cunningly makes Fortunato plead to go farther and farther into the catacombs by suggesting that they turn back and get Luchesi.

Montresor also shows his intelligence in his careful attention to details as he plans his revenge. By continuing to smile at gullible Fortunato, he does not let his victim know he is planning to kill him. He gets rid of witnesses. He finds a soundproof location to commit his crime. He lines the crypt with wine to keep Fortunato drunk. He prepares the crime scene—removing bones from one wall, installing chains, and getting bricks, mortar, and a trowel on site. Nothing is left undone as he prepares for the perfect murder.

Another indication of Montresor's intelligence is found in his clever use of puns and double meanings, as David S. Reynolds points out. Montresor plays on Fortunato's name, meaning the fortunate or lucky man, when they meet at the carnival. He says, "My dear Fortunato, you are luckily met" (667), when, of course, Fortunato is far from lucky. Another joke at Fortunato's expense occurs as the men are descending into the vaults and Fortunato dismisses his coughing by saying, "it will not kill me. I shall not die of a cough" (668). Montresor's seemingly innocent reply, "True—true" (668), is both humorous and ominous. When Fortunato drinks "to the buried that repose around us" (668), unwittingly toasting himself since he will soon be one of the dead, Montresor ironically responds, "and I to your long life" (669), knowing that Fortunato's hours are numbered (Reynolds, 106).

Other ironies are also found in this tale, including two used to foreshadow Fortunato's death. The first is the conversation about the Montresor coat of arms. Montresor sees the "huge human foot d'or [of gold], in a field azure" that "crushes a serpent rampant whose fangs are imbedded in the heel" (669) as a representation of himself because he will ultimately kill Fortunato, the serpent who has damaged him with biting insults. Another ironic foreshadowing takes place when the men converse about the Masons. When Fortunato scorns Montresor for claiming to be a Mason, which he regards as a member of the Masonic Order, Montresor produces a trowel, showing that he is a stonemason who erects things with bricks and mortar, specifically Fortunato's grave.

The names of the two men are also incongruous. *Fortunato* in Italian suggests "fortune," "fortunate," and "fated" (Thompson, *Selected Writings*, 417n3). However, "the fortunate one" is murdered because he is "fortunate" in having wealth and social prestige. His name further implies that he is part of the newly rich crowd, a man "who becomes rich and prominent by chance (Fortune), rather than through personal virtue" (Baraban, 52). *Montresor*, in French, "my treasure" (Thompson, *Selected Writings*, 417n3), has lost much of his treasure or wealth and, as a result, his social position. However, he does kill the person who fails to see the Montresor name as one to be "treasured."

Even the setting is ironic. The story takes place during the carnival season, a time of joy and merriment when the normal order of things is turned upside down. But Montresor twists the merry celebration into a sinister abandonment of social order as he commits murder. The carnival costumes worn by the two men ironically show their natures. Wealthy Fortunato, a foolish and gullible man, wears "motley," the clownish costume of a court fool. His costume even has a cap with bells that "jingle at key moments" to emphasize the foolishness of his actions: "when he first enters the catacombs; when he drinks the Médec; and after he has been completely walled in and has given up hope" (Reynolds, 105). Montresor is also dressed appropriately. Wearing a black silk mask and a cape, the traditional costume of a stage villain (Thompson, *Selected Writings*, 416n1), he looks like the murderer that he actually is.

Critics have pondered whether Montresor is a cold-blooded murderer or if he suffers from guilt. Three sentences in the last paragraph have led them to reach opposite conclusions about him: "My heart grew sick—on account of the dampness of the catacombs. . . . For the last half of a century no mortal has disturbed them. *In pace requiescat!*" (671). Some critics think that his statement, "For the half of a century no mortal has disturbed them" (671), shows that Montresor, now an old man who has been tormented by guilt for fifty years, is making a death-bed confession to receive absolution before he dies. For instance, Thompson theorizes that although "Montresor seems to be chuckling over his flawlessly executed revenge upon unfortunate Fortunato fifty years before . . . a moment's reflection suggests that the indistinct 'you' whom Montresor addresses in the first paragraph is probably his death-bed confessor. . . . We get the double effect of feeling the coldly calculated murder at the same time that we see the larger point that Montresor [has] suffered a fifty-years' ravage of conscience" (*Poe's Fiction*, 13–14).

However, since there is no internal evidence to prove that Montresor is either tormented or remorseful, the view of other critics—who regard Montresor as an unrepentant murderer who is bragging about his deed—seems more valid. Charles May points out that "even if our hypothesis that Montresor tells the story as a final confession . . . is correct, the tone or manner of his telling makes it clear that he has not atoned, for he enjoys himself in the telling too much—as much, in fact, as he did when he committed the crime itself" (81).

A second sentence that has received different interpretations is: "My heart grew sick—on account of the dampness of the catacombs" (671). Those who think Montresor is suffering from guilt argue that "fifty years later, he still remembers his heart's 'growing sick' . . . but his heartsickness likely arises from empathy with the man he is leaving to die amid that dampness" (Peeples, 150).

Although it is possible that this murderer felt a moment's twinge of conscience, it seems improbable that he has felt remorseful for fifty years since he gives no indication of regret. Furthermore, according to Baraban, Poe's use of a dash, which indicates a pause, in the middle of the sentence, shows "that Montresor feels satisfaction about his monstrous deed even after fifty years. The narrator is perfectly aware of the effect the second part of his sentence produces on his listener (even if the whole narration is Montresor's last confession and his listener is a priest). It destroys any hope in Montresor's humanity and highlights once again that Montresor feels no guilt regarding the murder" (49). Baraban concludes that "not only does Montresor feel no guilt, but he perceives his murder of Fortunato as a successful act of vengeance and punishment rather than crime" (49).

The last sentence, "*In pace requiescat!*" (671), has also puzzled commentators. These Latin words, translated "Rest in peace" (Thompson, *Selected Writings*, 421n7), are used as one of the last prayers at a burial service and during Last Rites when the priest forgives the sins of a dying person who has confessed. Those who see Montresor as a troubled sinner find these words ironic: "Fortunato had rested in peace for fifty years; Montresor must always have feared being found out" (Thomas O. Mabbott, quoted in Reynolds, 107). Those who see him as an unrepentant murderer claim that, by using these words, Montresor shows his arrogance: "If Montresor's narration is his last confession, he should look forward to being forgiven and to hearing *'In pace requiecas!'* [sic] ('May your soul rest in peace') from his priest. Instead, Montresor maliciously subverts his role as a repentant sinner when he says *'In pace requiescat!'* in regard to Fortunato. Not only does he deprive the poor man of a Catholic's right to the last confession, he is arrogant enough to abuse the formulaic expression used by priests to absolve dying sinners" (Baraban, 57). Therefore, Montresor remains a self-righteous murderer who "uses this expression for finally pardoning Fortunato [which] highlights his conviction that he has merely avenged himself for the wrong that Fortunato afflicted upon him fifty years ago" (57).

This tale, "a meditation on the art and passion of revenge" (Silverman, *Edgar A. Poe*, 316), is the story of a murderer who feels justified in his actions and proud of the way he accomplished the deed. Not a madman, he is the type of frightening human being who, as Buranelli writes, is "able to live quite well without a conscience" (72).

"The Fall of the House of Usher" (1839)

"The Fall of the House of Usher" is one of Poe's most famous gothic stories. It is filled with terrifying supernatural occurrences that put readers "in a position of horror, doubting both the world and the way we perceive it" (Howes, 40).

The narrator, having been invited to the home of his childhood friend, Roderick Usher, arrives at the gloomy, mysterious Usher estate. He sees a sinister reflection of the decaying mansion in a mountain lake, which Poe calls a tarn, and notices that there is a crack in the house that goes from the roof to the water. Inside the mansion, he finds his superstitious friend in an extremely nervous

THIS WOODCUT BY CONSTANT LE BRETON WAS CREATED FOR A
TWENTIETH-CENTURY EDITION OF "THE FALL OF THE HOUSE
OF USHER."

condition, suffering from a disease that has left him sensitive to lights and sounds. His sister, Madeline, is dying of catalepsy, "a nervous disorder related to epilepsy, schizophrenia, and hysteria in which the sufferer falls into a deep, narcotic sleep, has no response to external stimuli, shows no visible sign of breathing, and is stiff and rigid to the touch" (Thompson, *Selected Writings*, 205n8). Although the two friends paint and read together, Usher's mood does not improve. When Madeline dies, the narrator, helping Usher place his sister in the coffin and noticing that she looks just like Roderick, remembers they are twins. He also observes that her face still seems to blush with life. The men bury her in a basement vault and seal it with an iron door. Some nights later, a huge storm arises. To help calm Roderick, who is extremely agitated, the narrator reads aloud "Mad Trist," a medieval romance. The actions of the story are mimicked with noises coming from below, causing Roderick to shout that his sister was alive when they put her in her coffin. The door suddenly opens, and there stands Madeline. Weak after escaping from the coffin and the vault, she falls on her brother, and both immediately fall to the floor dead. As the frightened narrator runs from the house, the house breaks along the fissure and falls into the tarn.

In this frightening tale, Poe makes the setting seem ghostly and supernatural by filling the story with gothic elements: the old and decaying mansion is set in a remote countryside; inside are furtive servants and subterranean passages; both owners are afflicted with strange diseases; as a storm rages outside the castle, there are mysterious grating sounds inside; and a seemingly dead person comes back to life. All of these elements contribute to a fear of the unknown.

Poe develops his story by using pairings, two objects or people that mirror one another. By contrasting the attitudes of the narrator and Roderick Usher, Poe sets up two possible ways of viewing the world, either as a logical place governed by physical occurrences as seen by the rational narrator, or as a strange and mystical place run by supernatural influences as seen by Roderick Usher, who believes in supernatural "influences that seem to drive [him] . . . to madness, to kill him and Madeline, and even to destroy the House" (Bailey, 445).

At the beginning of the story, the narrator is a practical man who believes in a world that runs by explainable causes. A "rationalist and a skeptic regarding the supernatural—a man who habitually dismissed any explanation not in accord with commonplace fact" (Bailey, 445), the

narrator refuses to see the possibility of anything supernatural when he first observes the house. Therefore,
although he feels "a sense of insufferable gloom" (263)
and ponders "shadowy fancies" (263), he concludes that
"there *are* combinations of very simple natural objects
which have the power of thus affecting us" (263). The
narrator rejects his fear of the tarn as "superstition" and
"ridiculous" fancy (264), and he dismisses Roderick's suggestion that the House gives off an evil influence by thinking that his friend, filled with "nervous agitation" (263),
is insane.

As the story progresses, the narrator continues to
reject the supernatural as the cause of his growing uneasi-
ness, even though he cannot provide a logical explanation.
Thus, when Madeline's passing fills him with "utter aston-
ishment not unmingled with dread," he "found it impossible to account for such feelings" (267). Roderick's
strange music and paintings cause him to tremble, and he
"shuddered knowing not why" (268). He regards
Roderick's agitation after Madeline's burial as "the mere
inexplicable vagaries of madness" (272), and, when the
narrator becomes uneasy, he "struggled to reason off the
nervousness which had dominion over [him]" (273).
When the storm rages, he offers a reasonable explanation,
telling the frightened Roderick that it is "merely electrical
phenomena not uncommon—or it may be that they have
their ghastly origin in the rank miasma of the tarn" (274).
Thus, the rational narrator "explains away as nonexist-
ent, as illusion, or as superstition every phenomenon that
he considers unnatural or does not understand" (Bailey,
447).

However, at the end of the story, the once matter-of-
fact narrator flees "aghast" (276) from the house of Usher
as he witnesses seemingly supernatural incidences. As the
house sinks into the tarn, the narrator, as well as the reader, is left with a sense of horror, wondering whether the
house fell because of unexplainable occurrences or

because of natural events caused by "the combustion generated when the lightning of the storm crackles near the previously airless crypt—the inrushing electricity being conducted along the copper floor and igniting the remnants of powder" (Thompson, *Poe's Fiction*, 94). The horror, then, results from the nightmare of living in a world that is either irrational or terrifying.

Another pairing is the House of Usher, referring to "both the family and the family mansion" (264), which "are analogous stained with time, used up, crumbling from within, awaiting collapse" (Buranelli, 77). The total integration of the two is shown as the narrator compares Roderick and the mansion, first viewing one and then the other. He notes that both are cut off from civilization and are decaying. The aged mansion, discolored, overspread with fungi, and filled with crumbling individual stones, is located in some "dreary tract of country" (262) far away from people. Likewise, the ancient, inbred Usher family is falling apart, left with only the brother and sister, who both are sick. Because of the decay and isolation, both the people and the building are melancholy and gloomy. Roderick and the mansion are also both suffering from a type of splitting; the house has "a barely perceptible fissure, which, extending from the roof of the building in front, made its way down the wall in a zig-zag direction" (265), while Roderick's mind is split by a "mental disorder" (263) that threatens his sanity. At the end of the story, both the building and the man collapse.

A third paired image is found in the twins, Roderick and Madeline, who are alike in almost all ways. The narrator remarks on their "striking similitude" (272). He also notices that both appear to be dying, noting Roderick's "cadaverousness" and "ghastly pallor" (266) and observing that the lady Madeline is gradually wasting away from disease. Roderick, sick mentally, and Madeline, sick physically, represent the two inseparable parts of a person—the mind and the body. They are also considered representative of the two basic aspects of human beings—cold, rational thought, represented by Madeline, and unrestrained passion, represented by Roderick—which, when split apart, cause mutual destruction.

A number of critics suggest that the twins either have or desire to have a close, physical, incestuous relationship. However, the exact relationship between the brother and sister is left vague. As a result of this uncertainty, "the nature of Madeline's dying gesture is ambiguous. When Madeline falls inward on Roderick is it a fulfillment of their sensual passions? Or is her apparently violent gesture an act of blanketing generosity, an affirmation of their spiritual bond, a granting of her beloved brother's wish to merge with her?" (Kaplan, 63). Some critics see her as an "evil power" who, like a vampire, kills her brother (Bailey, 464). Others view her action as a culmination of incestuous love between the brother and sister who "loved each other passionately and exclusively" and therefore "must unite into unspeakable identification, oneness in death" (Lawrence, 99, 100). Still others see them as splintered parts of one being united in death; several see this unification as "the purification and reintegration of a soul" (Wilbur, 169), while different commentators write that they are united "tragically this time. The separation had gone to the extreme, disrupting the sentient balance, destroying both" (Timmerman, 243).

Many other paired images are also found in the story. The mansion is mirrored in the tarn. Roderick's painting of the underground burial vault parallels the burial chamber of Madeline. The poem, "The Haunted Palace," reflects the House of Usher "from a palace governed in orderly fashion by 'Thought's Dominion' to a den of disorder in which demons flicker about like bats—except that these demons are in Usher's mind" (Timmerman, 236). At the end of the tale, Poe parallels every action Ethelred takes to get into the hermit's home in "Mad

Trist" with Madeline's escape from the dungeon and entry into the room where the narrator and Roderick are sitting. Finally, the raging storm which surrounds the mansion is echoed in Roderick's collapsing mind.

Poe liked this story immensely and considered it one of his best tales (*Letters*, Vol. 1, 258). One of his contemporaries praised it, writing, "Had its author written nothing else, it would alone have been enough to stamp him as a man of genius, and the master of a classic style" (Lowell, 15). Later critics and readers agree, many finding it "to be one of *the* greatest short stories in all of world literature. Few would disagree, at least, that it is one of Poe's most popular and justifiably famous works" (Burduck, 1).

"The Masque of the Red Death" (1842)

"The Masque of the Red Death" is an allegory, a story told with symbols, to teach the message that death is inevitable and that humans are powerless to defy it.

Wishing to avoid a deadly plague devastating the country, Prince Prospero summons a thousand knights and ladies to his castle to be lavishly entertained while they wait for death to pass them by. After months of carousing, the Prince holds a masked ball in seven unusual rooms of his castle, each one lit by a different color light that comes through the stained glass windows. The last room, the westernmost one, is bathed in red light and decorated in black. A strange ebony clock in the room ominously strikes periodically, causing the orchestra to stop playing as everyone listens to the chimes. At midnight, a figure, masked like a corpse and sprinkled all over with blood, appears and terrifies everyone. Furious that someone would wear the costume of the Red Death, Prospero follows him from room to room, ending in the black-and-red one. As the prince raises his dagger to kill the guest, Prospero falls dead. When the other revelers enter the room, they also die.

Poe begins this story by using words that establish feelings of horror and fear of death as he describes the plague: "devastated," "pestilence," "fatal," "hideous," "Blood," "horror of blood," "sharp pains," "sudden dizziness," "profuse bleeding at the pores," "dissolution," "scarlet stains," "pest ban," and "disease" (384). He ends on a note of fear as well, repeating the sound of the letter *d* to help show the finality of death: "And Darkness and Decay and the Red Death held illimitable dominion over all" (388).

Because it is an allegory, the story is filled with symbols. The seven rooms, arranged from east to west, like the movement of the sun, represent the passing of time as a person moves from birth to youth to old age and finally to death. The last room, symbolic of death, is described as if it were dead: the ceiling, walls, and carpet are "shrouded" (385) in black, and the windows are "scarlet—a deep blood color" (385). The ebony clock that chimes portentously every hour marks the passage of time and the approach of death, a point Poe reinforces by emphasizing the length of time: each hour strikes "after the lapse of sixty minutes (which embrace three thousand and six hundred seconds of the Time that flies)" (386).

The characters are also allegorical. Prince Prospero is not only a person in the story, but he represents happy, prosperous people who, when faced with death, care only for themselves and their select friends. Having no concern for his dying peasants, he lets his fear of death wipe out all other feelings as he walls himself and his thousand friends in an elaborate castle to escape death. His folly is revealed when the Red Death participates in his masked ball.

The Red Death is also a character as well as the symbol of physical death. Everything about him suggests death. He is a "spectral image"; his "tall and gaunt" body is "shrouded" in grave clothes, while his mask looks like "a stiffened corpse"; sprinkled all over is blood, "the scarlet horror"; as he "stalked" among the revelers, his movements are "slow and solemn," "deliberate and stately" (387–388). The appearance of death first brings out the people's feelings "of terror, of horror, and of disgust" (387), which later turn into "deadly terror" (388) of the Red Death who "had come like a thief in the night" (388), a biblical reference to death. Saint Paul writes, "For you yourselves know well that the day of the Lord will come like a thief in the night. When people say, 'There is peace and security,' then sudden destruction will come upon them . . . and there will be no escape" (1 Thessalonians 5:2–3). Saint Peter repeats this idea: "But the day of the Lord will come like a thief, and then the heavens will pass away with a loud noise, and the elements will be dissolved with fire, and the earth and the works that are upon it will be burned up" (2 Peter 3:10).

This successful story creates a mood of fear and horror of death from which no one can escape.

"The Murders in the Rue Morgue" (1841)

When Poe wrote his groundbreaking tale, "The Murders in the Rue Morgue," he invented the detective story. The focus of this tale of ratiocination, like his two later detective tales, is the relationship between the incompetent Paris police and the brilliant private investigator.

After describing the types of minds that do well at chess and draughts (checkers), the narrator relates how he first met C. Auguste Dupin, a scholarly, imaginative young man who is good at analysis. A short time later, the two men read a newspaper account of the horrific murders of Madame L'Espanaye and her daughter. Neighbors, waking to the shrieks of the victims, heard two voices, a Frenchman and a shrill voice speaking in an unknown language. When the neighbors and police forced open the locked door, they found the room torn apart and strewn

AN ORANGUTAN ATTACKS A WOMAN AND PULLS HER HAIR IN THIS ILLUSTRATION OF THE MURDER SCENE IN "THE MURDERS IN THE RUE MORGUE."

with gold, which had been delivered by a bank clerk three days earlier. The mother's beaten and nearly decapitated body was found in the backyard while the corpse of the strangled daughter was found in the chimney.

When the police mistakenly arrest the bank teller for the murders, Dupin decides to solve the crime. After he examines the crime scene, he discusses the case with the narrator and summarizes the situation. He notes that the killer spoke in a shrill voice in an unrecognizable language, departed from the room by a window fastened by a concealed spring, swung to a lightning rod, and climbed down. Although he did not rob the women, he committed a murder that was inhumanly brutal. When the narrator incorrectly concludes that the murderer was an escaped madman, Dupin, showing him nonhuman hair that he found in Madame L'Espanaye's fingers and pointing out the nonhuman finger marks on the daughter's neck, tells the narrator that an "ourang-outang" (orangutan) committed the murders. To find the owner, Dupin places an advertisement in the newspaper saying that he has found the animal. Soon, a sailor comes to Dupin's house to claim his pet, and, at Dupin's demand, tells what he knows about the murders. The sailor says that the animal, holding a razor, escaped from his apartment. He followed it and watched it climb the lightning rod to the L'Espanaye window and kill the women before escaping. The sailor later finds his pet and sells it for a large amount of money, and the police, told of Dupin's solution to the crime, release the bank teller.

In this first of three detective stories ("The Mystery of Marie Rogêt," 1842–1843, and "The Purloined Letter," 1844, follow), Poe creates his central crime-solving character, C. Auguste Dupin, a highly intelligent, reclusive gentleman who is interested in literature and even writes some poetry. He has a sidekick of average intelligence, the narrator, who needs Dupin to explain to him what has actually happened and then passes the information on to the reader. Dupin knows the police and the Paris prefect, an ineffectual investigator who uses ordinary, unimaginative police methods to try to solve crimes and then, when he is unsuccessful, calls on Dupin for help. Dupin, using both his powers of imagination as a poet and the powers of reason like a mathematician, analyzes the crime, dismisses unimportant information, and pieces together the essential facts to solve it.

The story is organized in three sections, headed by an epigraph from a seventeenth-century writer. The quote, "What song the Syrens sang, or what name Achilles assumed when he hid himself among women, although puzzling questions, are not beyond *all* conjecture" (315), refers to two questions an emperor asks of scholars, questions that, although difficult, can be solved (Thompson, *Selected Writings*, 240n1). This quote effectively sets up the story of a difficult crime that has baffled the police but which can be solved by an intuitive, reasoning thinker.

Poe begins his tale with a long, two-part introduction. The first is a philosophical discussion about the types of people who play draughts and chess, which ends by proving that draughts players are superior to chess players because draughts requires both intuition and analysis (315–317). In the second part of the introduction, the narrator explains how he met Dupin and describes him, concluding with a demonstration of Dupin's ability to intuitively know the narrator's thoughts (317–320). Dupin is a mindreader who, as Daniel Hoffman explains, does not use telepathy or supernatural powers, but rather "works by association," retracing "the probable chain of associations likely to occur to Narrator after his being jostled by a fruiterer . . . [to] then propose the *exact words* likely to be in his companion's mind" (107).

The second part of the story concerns the murders in the Rue Morgue, beginning with newspaper accounts, then moving to Dupin's reflections on the facts of the case, and ending with his announcement that the crime was committed by an "ourang-outang" (326–335). The third section explains how the murders occurred as Dupin, using his power of reasoning to identify the animal's owner, entices him to appear and tell the story of the murders. With Dupin's theory confirmed, the falsely accused bank clerk is set free (335–341). The story concludes with Dupin's criticism of the prefect's inability to solve the crime because he cannot analyze accurately since the prefect, as Dupin says in French, operates by "denying what is, and explaining what is not" (Thompson, *Selected Writings*, 266n3).

With this story, Poe introduced the first intelligent, eccentric detective who solves difficult crimes by thinking both rationally and intuitively, and he created a new genre—detective stories.

"The Pit and the Pendulum" (1842)

In "The Pit and the Pendulum," another horror story, "Poe created an image of suffering palpable enough to terrify generations of readers" (Malloy, 95).

The story opens as the narrator tells how he fainted after he was sentenced to death during the Inquisition in Toledo. When he wakes up, he is terrified to find himself in total darkness. Deciding to examine his jail cell, he slowly inches his way around the dungeon. Soon he is overcome with fatigue and sleep. When he wakes up a second time, he eats the food and water left beside him, and resumes his walk around the cell, determining that the cell is about one hundred paces around. He next decides to walk across the cell, but, luckily, trips and falls on the slimy floor just before he steps into a water-filled pit in the center of the dungeon. Once again, he sleeps.

When he awakens, he ravenously devours the bread and water placed next to him, and falls into another deep sleep. The next time he is conscious, he finds himself tied face up on a wooden frame. Now, with a ray of light in the room, he can see rats running around him and a moving pendulum with a sharp blade swinging over his body, getting closer and closer to his chest. As the pendulum is beginning to slice into his robe, he smears food on the ropes and lets the rats crawl over him to gnaw the ropes and free him. As soon as he escapes from the pendulum, the iron walls of his cell grow hot and move inward, pushing him closer and closer to the open pit. Just as he is about to fall into it, he hears voices, a trumpet blast, and harsh gratings. The fiery walls rush back, and General Lasalle rescues him.

Unlike most of Poe's horror stories, this one is set in a real city at a real time with a real rescuer, making the depravity of humans who devise such forms of torture seem extremely terrifying and horrendous. It takes place during the Spanish Inquisition, which lasted from 1478 to 1834, and was started to punish heretics, usually by public executions. The narrator's rescuer, General Lasalle, one of Napoleon's generals, entered the city of Toledo in 1808, the year Poe's story takes place (Thompson, *Selected Writings*, 305n2).

Poe immediately establishes the tone of fear and horror by using words relating to sickness, pain, and death: "I was sick—sick unto death," "long agony," "my senses were leaving me," "the dread sentence of death," "black-robed judges," "deadly locution," "delirious horror," "deadly nausea," and "a mad rushing descent as of the soul into Hades" (434–435). Numerous words expressing horror, terror, and agonizing death continue throughout the story.

To further create the sense of horror, Poe uses apocalyptic imagery, symbols that relate to the end of the world. In the opening paragraph, the candles, fire, and angels relate to the apocalyptic Book of Revelation, in which Saint John tells his vision of the final days of the earth: "I saw seven golden lampstands, and in the midst of the lampstands one like a son of man; . . . his eyes were like a flame of fire" (Rev. 1:12–14). In the story, the narrator sees seven candles on a table that first "wore the aspect of charity, and seemed white slender angels who would save me," but almost immediately "the angel forms became meaningless specters with heads of flame, and I saw that from them there would be no help" (434). As Jeanne M. Malloy points out, "By beginning the tale with the narrator's trial and death sentence and by couching these events in apocalyptic imagery, Poe heralds the narrator's, and hence the reader's, entrance into a nightmare world of punishment, dissolution, and death, an announcement amply fulfilled by the violence, pain, and horror experienced by the narrator in his prison cell" (82–83).

However, as Malloy further explains, "the Book of Revelation also sets forth the promise of salvation, the eternal life granted the faithful. Despite its depiction of the present age as given over to the forces of evil, Revelation proclaims that judgment and the destruction of the world will be followed by the creation of a new heaven and a new earth (21:1)" (83). Poe's tale concludes with images that relate to the Second Coming of Christ who delivers the faithful. There is "a loud blast as of many trumpets," "a thousand thunders," "fiery walls," and an "outstretched arm" that saves the prisoner (445).

This story demonstrates that human life consists of terrible suffering caused by the maliciousness of other people. James Lundquist accurately summarizes the situation: "The anonymous hero condemned for an unknown, or at least unstated, crime by a merciless [sic] Inquisition apparently represents mankind condemned by a vindictive power for an almost forgotten sin. His sentence is not immediate death but life lived amid horror" (quoted in Malloy, 89). The terrified prisoner is tortured psychologically until his "nerves had been unstrung" (438); he "grew frantically mad" (440); and he thinks that "long suffering had nearly annihilated all my ordinary powers of mind" (441).

The prisoner is a very intelligent man who is able to avoid death for a short time. When he accidentally discovers the pit, instead of seeing it as a means of a quick death by drowning, he focuses on information he has read about pits, "that the *sudden* extinction of life formed no part of their most horrible plan" (438). Therefore, he avoids the pit, knowing that he would slowly die of torture at the bottom of the hole. Later, he brilliantly escapes from the pendulum by getting the rats to eat the ropes that hold him. But he realizes he "had but escaped death in one form of agony, to be delivered unto worse than death in some other" (443). At the end, all he can do is choose either to fall into the pit to be tortured or to burn alive in the fiery walls. G. R. Thompson calls this story "one of Poe's clearest dramatizations of the futile efforts of man's will to survive the malevolent perversity of the world and to make order out of chaos" (*Poe's Fiction*, 171).

"The Purloined Letter" (1844)

A "masterpiece of ratiocination" (Hoffman, 132), "The Purloined Letter," Poe's third and most famous detective story, is different from his first tales of ratiocination because it has less action and more intellectual analysis.

While the narrator is visiting C. Auguste Dupin, the prefect of the Paris police arrives to get Dupin's advice about a case. He tells him that an important government officer, Minister D-----, has stolen a letter from a lady, giving him immense political power over her. Although she knows he has the letter, she cannot take any action against him, but she needs to get the letter back. However, the prefect cannot find the letter even though he and his men have searched diligently. Dupin advises him to conduct a new search. A month later, the depressed prefect returns.

When he hires Dupin to retrieve the letter, Dupin hands it to him. He then tells the narrator how he got the letter. He imaginatively tried to think like Minister D-----. Knowing that the minister would need to have the letter readily available and that the police would conduct a typical search, Dupin realized the thief would hide the letter in an obvious place. To check his theory, Dupin visited the minister and noticed the missing letter, readdressed to himself, sitting on his desk. Leaving his snuffbox behind, Dupin departed. After arranging for someone to create a disturbance on the streets, he returned the following day to get his snuffbox. When the host was distracted by the street noise, Dupin took the purloined letter and replaced it with an imitation, which contained a hidden message for the minister, who had once insulted him.

The story, structured in two halves, is introduced by an epigraph written in Latin that means, "Nothing is more hateful to sense than too much cunning" (Thompson, *Selected Writings*, 367n 2). This saying introduces the way Dupin will rationally and intuitively analyze the situation and solve the problem by using psychology. The first half of the story consists of two visits by the Parisian prefect of police and ends as Dupin produces the letter and the policeman gives him his reward money.

In the second half of the tale, Dupin tells the narrator how he solved the case by using psychology to understand the Minister and by making two visits to the Minister's house. The story concludes with a quote that Dupin left in the letter, words that will identify him as the person who got revenge on the Minister for once insulting him. Found in a play, *Atrée et Thyeste*, written by Prosper Jolyot de Crébillon, the words in English mean, "So malevolent a plan, if unworthy of Atreus, is yet worthy of Thyestes" (Thompson, *Selected Writings*, 382n2). In the play, Thyestes begins a conflict with his brother Atreus by seducing his wife. In revenge, Atreus kills Thyestes's sons, cooks them, and serves them to Thyestes. Dupin implies that even though his revenge is not as horrific as Atreus's, it is as clever as Thyestes's.

Dupin is, thus, seen as the ideal detective: he is able to solve crimes the police cannot because he knows how

"THE TELL-TALE HEART" IS ONE OF POE'S SCARIEST TALES.

to use psychology to get into the mind of the criminal; he is a savior to the oppressed; and he achieves perfect revenge on a person who has wronged him.

"The Tell-Tale Heart" (1843)

"The Tell-Tale Heart," considered "one of his nearly perfect tales" (Hoffman, 221–222), is Poe's most famous psychotic tale. It is told by a murderer who attempts to prove his sanity as he describes how he killed an old man he professes to love.

Claiming that he is nervous but not insane, the narrator says he has a disease that has sharpened his senses, particularly his sense of hearing. To prove his sanity, he tells his story, showing how he carefully and wisely carries out his intentions to kill the old man because of his filmy, vulturelike blue eye. For seven nights, he sneaks into the old man's room when he is sleeping. At midnight on the eighth night, he once again creeps into the room. This time the old man wakes up and cries out in terror. For an hour, he sits up in his bed, while the narrator waits quietly at the door. Finally, the narrator opens his lantern a crack and lets a ray of light fall on the man's bad eye. When the old man's heart begins pounding, the narrator jumps on his victim, drags the bed on top of him, and kills him. Then, he dismembers the body, carefully catching all the blood in a tub, and buries him under three floor boards.

At 4:00 a.m., three policemen arrive, investigating a complaint that someone screamed. Totally confident, the narrator lets the officers in, says that he yelled in a dream, and shows them the room of the old man, who, he claims, is on a trip. As the policemen stay to chat, the narrator places chairs on top of the floorboards containing the body. Hearing ringing in his ears, the narrator talks vigorously and paces in the room, but the officers only smile. The sound becomes a pounding that grows louder and louder. Certain that they can hear the old man's heart beating, the narrator shrieks that he killed the old man.

Strangely, the murderer is not concerned with proving his innocence, only his sanity. His argument is that "madness is incompatible with systematic action, and as evidence of his capacity for the latter he relates how he has executed a horrible crime with rational precision" (Robinson, 369). Early in the story, he introduces his argument: "You fancy me mad. Madmen know nothing. But you should have seen *me*. You should have seen how wisely I proceeded—with what caution—with what foresight—with what dissimulation I went to work!" (445). However, as he tells the story of the brutal murder and dismemberment he carried out, the reader realizes that he is indeed crazy. His motive, killing a harmless old man because of a bad eye, is not a rational one. Furthermore, the narrator himself seems to grab this as an excuse because he initially says, "it is impossible to say how first the idea entered my brain" (445). After he goes on to explain that there was no object, no passion, no desire for revenge, no wish for money, he hits upon an excuse: "I think it was his eye! Yes, it was this!" (445).

Another way Poe reveals his character's insanity is the narrator's claim that he is acutely sensitive to sight and sound, a fact he ironically offers as further proof of his sanity. He views his hypersensitivity as a normal outcome of a disease that, he claims, "sharpened my senses—not destroyed—not dulled them" (445). He thinks his sensitivity to sight causes him to obsess about the old man's "pale blue eye, with a film over it" (445). It bothers him so much that he irrationally decides he must kill the old man. Night after night, he haunts the old man, letting a thin ray of light escape from his lantern just so he can see the "vulture" eye (445). But for seven nights, the eye is closed, so the narrator does nothing. However, on the eighth night, the eye is wide open and the narrator murders him in a wild frenzy. Everything about his obsession is strange; it is not the attitude of a sane man.

Even more important to the narrator than his heightened sense of sight is his acute sense of hearing. Each time he hears something, he acts more like a madman. When he hears the old man groan with terror on the eighth night of his stalking, he "chuckled at heart" (446). A little later, he hears the old man's heart beating, which, he says, "increased my fury" (447). As "the hellish tattoo of the heart increased," the narrator is "excited . . . to uncontrollable terror" (447). When the police come, the old man's heart beats louder and louder, until the narrator is frantic, describing himself as a madman: "I foamed—I raved—I swore" (448). Finally, he irrationally shrieks, "Villains! . . . dissemble no more! I admit the deed!—tear up the planks!—here, here!—it is the beating of his hideous heart" (448). Ironically, the narrator thinks that because he has a superior sense of hearing, he hears the old man's heart beating, but he is really only listening to his own pounding heart, a situation which gives the title "a new significance: the 'tell-tale' heart belongs to him who tells this tale!" (Howarth, 11).

Even though it is clear that the narrator is insane as he kills the old man and confesses to the policemen, it is not his madness that causes him to tell his story to the unnamed listener. It seems he does this because he is "an egocentric who derives pleasure from cruelty" (Pritchard, 144). Hollie Pritchard notices that he is proud of his crime, bragging about "how healthily—how calmly [he] can tell you the whole story" (445), delighting in his power over the old man so that he "could scarcely contain [his] feelings of triumph" (446), taking pleasure in finally feeling "the extent of [his] own powers—of [his] sagacity" (446), and congratulating himself for committing the perfect crime (445). Pritchard concludes that he tells his tale "so that it can be immortalized in ink. Knowing that his story will live on is the final step that the narrator must take to receive pleasure from his cruelty" (446).

This story is an insightful study of the deep depravity of human beings.

Literary Criticism of Poe's Tales

Although the response to Poe's short stories, in general, has been enthusiastic, his tales have often not been appreciated as serious works of literature, especially in America.

The reviews of Poe's first collection of stories, *Tales of the Grotesque and the Arabesque*, published in 1839, were positive. One critic praised him for his great intellect, vivid descriptions, magnificent imagination, and elegant diction, writing that "had Mr. Poe written nothing else but 'Morella,' 'William Wilson,' 'The House of Usher,' and the "MS Found in a Bottle,' he would deserve a high place among imaginative writers" (Tasistro, 36). Poe was also admired by some major authors of the day. For example, Henry Wadsworth Longfellow wrote to Poe that "you are destined to stand among the first romance-writers of the country, if such be your aim" (quoted in A. H. Quinn, 317). Margaret Fuller found his stories "refreshing" because they are "the fruit of genuine observations and experience" ("[Review of *Tales*]," 36–37). Poet James Russell Lowell praised Poe's short stories, writing that Poe had "two faculties which are seldom found united; a power of influencing the mind of the reader by the impalpable shadows of mystery, and a minuteness of detail which does not leave a pin, or a button unnoticed" (13). Even Rufus Griswold recognized Poe's skills as a short-story writer, declaring that in tale writing, Poe "was henceforth alone and unapproachable" and that two of his tales "have the unquestionable stamp of genius" (52). Although his short stories were praised in America, Poe was not considered one of the great writers of the age.

However, contemporary French authors were extremely enthusiastic about Poe's stories. An early supporter, E. D. Forgues, reviewing Poe's *Tales* in 1846, treated Poe as a serious writer and helped establish Poe's high reputation in Europe, an appreciation that continued after his death. In 1857, Charles Baudelaire hailed Poe as a writer who "was always great" because of "his noble conceptions" and his ability to see and affirm "the natural perversity of man" (65–66). In the early twentieth century, dramatist George Bernard Shaw announced that "in his stories of mystery and imagination Poe created a world-record for the English language: perhaps for all the languages" (89), while fiction writer D. H. Lawrence was impressed with Poe's ability to show the "first vivid, seething reduction of the psyche" (91).

Traditionally, Europeans have held Poe in higher esteem than critics in the United States. In the first hundred years after his death, Poe was dismissed as a serious writer by some major U.S. authors. Henry James, writing in the late nineteenth century, alleged that "to take him with more than a certain degree of seriousness is to lack seriousness in one's self" (66), while in the mid-twentieth century, T. S. Eliot declared that, although Poe's tales "had great influence upon some types of popular fiction," his works are no longer important because readers are not "capable of being thrilled" by them (208).

However, since World War II, Poe's stories have received much critical attention in the United States and have been analyzed over and over again in numerous scholarly publications and books. In addition, critics have recognized his great influence on other writers of detective stories. His hero, C. Auguste Dupin, is "a model for the detective that continues to dominate mystery writing. Dupin's eccentric personality and especially his relation to his two foils—a sympathetic but naïve narrator, nameless throughout the series, and an unsympathetic professional investigator, the Prefect of Police Monsieur G.—were explicitly reproduced in such detectives as Arthur Conan Doyle's Sherlock Holmes, Rex Stout's Nero Wolfe, and Agatha Christie's Hercule Poirot" (Van Leer, 65).

Poe's reputation has risen in the United States so that today he is recognized as a leading short-story writer.

Chapter 4

Poe's Poetry

POE "WAS, IN HIS OWN ESTIMATE OF HIMSELF, and in fact, essentially a poet, and remained so to the end of his life" (Stovall, 262), beginning and ending his career by publishing poetry. *Tamerlane and Other Poems*, printed in 1827 when Poe was only eighteen, was followed by *Al Aaraaf, Tamerlane, and Minor Poems* in 1829 and *Poems* in 1831. Immediately after his death, "Annabel Lee" and "The Bells" were published. Between these years, he wrote in other genres in order to pay his bills, even though he says in his 1845 "Preface to *The Raven and Other Poems*" that he would have preferred to write only poetry. "Events not to be controlled have prevented me from making, at any time, any serious effort in what, under happier circumstances, would have been the field of my choice. With me poetry has been not a purpose, but a passion; and the passions should be held in reverence" (978).

Poe held definite views about the nature of poetry, expressing them in his book reviews and in three long essays—"The Rationale of Verse" (1843), "The Philosophy of Composition" (1846), and "The Poetic Principle" (1850). In "The Poetic Principle," he defines poetry as *"The Rhythmical Creation of Beauty,"* declaring that music is an essential element in poetry and that the "contemplation of the Beautiful" is its only function (1027). Since poetry is not a teaching device, he believed it "has no concern whatever either with Duty or with Truth" (1027), although he did admit that "the incitements of Passion, or the precepts of Duty, or even the lessons of Truth" could be introduced into a poem as long as they are toned down "in proper subjection to the Beauty" (1027). In order to achieve one effect, which is *"an elevating excitement of the soul"* (1039), a poem must be brief (1021–1023) and must have a sad or melancholy tone because "sadness is inseparably connected" to beauty (1030). In all forty-eight of his published poems, Poe tries to follow his rules.

Several of them, including "Annabel Lee," "The Bells," "Eldorado," and "The Raven," are repeatedly anthologized and studied in high school and college classes around the country. These four popular poems will be discussed here.

"Annabel Lee" (1849)

This poem of youthful love that lasts beyond death tells the story of a beautiful maiden named Annabel Lee who is dearly loved by the poet. When they were children, they loved each other "with a love that was more than love" (9) in a kingdom by the sea. Such exceeding love makes the angels envious, and they send a wind that chills and kills the lovely young girl, who is carried away by her kin and buried by the sea. The poet vows that nothing, not even angels or demons, can separate their souls. Every night he dreams of her and sees her eyes in the stars. The poem closes as he lies by her tomb and is with her spiritually.

"Annabel Lee" is a type of ballad, a poem that relates a story of love or death, and is written in a modified ballad style. Instead of the ballad's typical four-line stanzas, Poe's poem consists of six stanzas of varying length—three stanzas with six lines, one with seven, and two with eight. However, the meter is the characteristic ballad rhythm of alternating lines of tetrameter and trimeter, made up of both iambs (a two-syllable foot consisting of one unaccented and one accented syllable) and anapests (a foot consisting of three syllables—two unaccented and one accented). Poe rhymes alternate lines, with a few variations in the last two stanzas, by using only the words "Lee," "sea," "me," and "we," a technique that produces a type of refrain. Periodically, he includes internal rhyme to help portray a mood. For example, the rhyming words "chilling and killing" (26) stress the sudden and cruel end of Annabel Lee's life, and "ever dissever" (32) help show the permanence of their love. In the last stanza, Poe uses the rhymes "beams/dreams" (34), "rise/eyes" (36), and "night-tide/the side" (38) to help emphasize the ongoing presence of Annabel Lee.

Poe's choice of diction helps evoke the mood. The narrator and Annabel Lee's total love for one another is depicted as "happily ever after," the type of true love found in fairy tales. Like a fairy tale, which often begins with the words, "Once upon a time in a kingdom far away," Poe sets his poem in the far past, "It was many and many a year ago" (1), and in an unnamed kingdom, "In a kingdom by the sea" (2). His diction also helps define the purity of their love as he refers to Annabel Lee, not as a "woman," but as a "maiden" (3, 5), a word that suggests purity and youth.

Which woman inspired this poignant love poem is uncertain. Although people have claimed that it was written about Annie Richmond, Sarah Helen Whitman, or Fanny Osgood, Osgood herself was convinced it was written about Virginia (A. H. Quinn, 606). Perhaps Silverman is correct when he claims that "Annabel Lee represents all of the women he loved and lost" (*Edgar A. Poe*, 402).

Although "Annabel Lee" "has been the most popular of the late short poems," it has not been praised by critics, who "often dismiss it as meaningless or damn it with faint praise for its alleged 'simple' melody" (Stovall, 225).

"The Bells" (1849)

This four-stanza poem describes four types of bells. In the cold night air, silver bells found on snow sleighs tinkle merrily. Next, golden wedding bells, ringing in the balmy night air, foretell a long, happy future. Then brazen alarum bells clamor during the night as they ring out the horrors and dangers of life. Finally, in the silence of the night, solemn funeral bells toll a death.

Kenneth Silverman considers "The Bells" to be one of Poe's "most despairing" poems (*Edgar A. Poe*, 403). Poe progresses through the four stages of life, moving from the gaiety of childhood found in cheery sleigh bells, to the happy wedding bells of youth, to frightening alarum bells of middle age, to tolling bells of old age ending in death. "In mounting frenzy and verbal discord, the happiness foretold by the sleigh bells and wedding bells is revealed as a cheat, the insignificant preliminary to an onslaught of annihilation. . . . Poe depicted existence as the plaything of a lying, sadistic Overlord of Life, the Banquet of a Ghoul–God" (*Edgar A. Poe*, 403–404).

One way Poe develops the mood of despair is by making each stanza longer than the previous one. The happy silver bells (14 lines) and the golden bells of marriage (21 lines) take up less than one-third of the 112-line poem. The other 77 lines—34 in stanza three and 43 in stanza four—are devoted to the horrors of middle age and the finality of death.

Probably more than any other of Poe's poems, "The Bells" uses sounds, both vowels and consonants, to convey its meaning. For example, A. H. Quinn explains that the silvery sound of the sleigh bells is echoed by the closed vowels in these words: "How they tinkle, tinkle, tinkle, / In the icy air of night!" (4–5), while the stars "oversprinkle" (6) and the heavens "twinkle" (7). The golden wedding bells strike mellow tones that are mimicked by the open vowels: "Hear the mellow wedding bells— / Golden Bells!" (15–16) (A. H. Quinn, 564).

Poe also effectively uses consonants by employing both alliteration, the repetition of initial consonant sounds, and consonance, the recurrence of similar consonant sounds in close proximity. The lighthearted feeling produced by the silver sleigh bells is mimicked with words containing the letter "m" which produces a sound of pleasure, "Mmmmm": "What a world of merriment their melody foretells!" (3). The marriage bells, which bring long-lasting happiness, repeat the breathy *h* to add to the feeling of serenity: "What a world of happiness their harmony foretells" (17). As pleasure gives way to the pain of middle age in the third stanza, the harsh sound of the *t* spits out the sense of horror and despair: "What a tale of terror, now, their turbulency tells" (38). Throughout this verse, Poe also selects words containing two other explosive consonants, *k* and *d*, adding to the feelings of discord—"scream" (40), "shriek, shriek" (41), "clamorous" (44), "clang and clash" (54), "clamor," "clangor" (69), "deaf" (45), "desperate desire" (47), and "despair" (53). In the fourth stanza, the funeral bells seem more melancholy because of the repetition of *s* and *l*, sounds that imitate those made when a person is languishing or moaning: "What a world of solemn thought their monody compels!" (72). In this final stanza, the words with double *l*s make the mood very somber: "tolling" (70, 82, 109), "tolls" (89, 90), "rolling" (107), "rolls" (90), "knells" (105), and "bells," used twenty-three times.

Although some readers do not appreciate Poe's techniques in this poem, including critic Anthony Caputi, who calls "The Bells" Poe's "most colossal failure" (176), others marvel at the poet's total control of alliteration, onomatopoeia (a word formed from its sound), and tintinnabulation (ringing and tinkling sounds), which Poe uses to make the sleigh bells light and merry. Quinn, for instance, calls it "one of the most successful verbal imitations of sound in the English language" (564), while Kevin Graham writes that "if Poe aimed to produce an effect, he was most certainly successful with 'The Bells'" (11). Vincent Buranelli also praises it as "one of his most remarkable successes," adding that "world literature can scarcely show a more triumphant handling of onomatopoeia—suggestiveness and meaning conveyed through the medium of sounds" (108).

"Eldorado" (1849)

This four-stanza poem tells the story of a gaily dressed knight singing while searching for Eldorado, the city of gold. In the second stanza, the knight, growing old, becomes sad because he has not found anything that could be Eldorado. As his strength fails him in stanza three, he meets a pilgrim shadow and asks it where he can find Eldorado. In the last stanza, the shade tells him to ride boldly over the mountains of the moon and down the valley of the shadow if he wishes to find Eldorado.

The name *Eldorado* comes from the mythical city made of gold that Spanish conquistadors searched for but never found. According to G. R. Thompson, the name was originally given to an Indian king in Colombia who, after covering himself in gold, was called "El Dorado," meaning "the gilded one." He also decorated everything in his capitol city with gold. Thompson notes that *Eldorado* in Poe's time was a nickname for California, the state of the gold rush (*Selected Writings*, 74n1). The name also developed wider connotations, meaning "the far-off land of gold, sometimes with over-tones of philosophical bliss" (Buranelli, 107).

In form, the poem is simple, consisting of four six-line stanzas, each one following an aabccb rhyme scheme. Since all *b* rhymes are composed of only two words, "shadow" and "Eldorado," Poe creates a type of refrain. After a casual reading, the poem's meaning also seems simple; however, the poem, in reality, is not easily interpreted. Some critics find it an optimistic work while others argue that it is pessimistic.

In the early twentieth century, most commentators viewed it as an optimistic poem encouraging people to search for an ideal. Critics wrote that it reflected "the unconquerable idealism of the poet and the idealism of the nation whose fame he carried into all lands" (Smith, 248–249). It has been called "finely emblematic of Poe's own faith and aspirations" (Campbell, 286), "the quest of human happiness in which man never tires," "a noble expression of the ideal as Poe sought it, and as all men, to some extent at least, also seek it" (Alterton and Craig, 507), and a representation of "Poe's ideality" (Clark, 844). As recently as 1961, Eric W. Carlson regarded "Eldorado" as "another expression of Poe's lifelong attachment to an absolute ideal" ("Poe's 'Eldorado,'" 233).

The views during the 1940s, when World War II was raging, were almost as optimistic. Even though critics pointed out that the quest for gold might lead to death, they felt that those seeking the ideal died happily. Oral Sumner Coad wrote that Poe "used the mythical Eldorado, suggested by the gold rush of 1849, to symbolize death, the land of gold for him," a courageous type of death which is "an Eden" (60, 61). This was echoed by Thomas O. Mabbott, who explained that Poe used the symbol of Eldorado, referring to the California gold rush, to show "that many who hastened to California would find there not gold, but disappointment and death, a terrible but not necessarily unhappy meeting. Those who ride *boldly*, even with all odds against them, can find the Valley of the Moon" (312, 314).

However, in the second half of the twentieth century, the poem has often been viewed as a pessimistic allegory about the disillusionment of an idealist. The changing meanings of the word *shadow* reveal the lack of value of the knight's career. First, the word means shade; in the second stanza, it is gloom and doubt; then it is a ghost; and in the fourth stanza, it is a symbol of death. In the last stanza, the shade implies that the knight will not succeed in his quest. First, he suggests that the knight's search for the ideal will be in vain as he instructs him to ride "'Over the Mountains / Of the Moon" (19–20), a reference to "the snow-laden Montes Lunae of antiquity, long considered legendary, here meant to suggest something impossibly far away" (Thompson, *Selected Writings*, 74n2). As W. Stephen Sanderlin Jr. points out, the reference seems to suggest "a doubt concerning the eventual success of his knight who is advised to make a journey in regions the very existence of which is open to question" (191). Second, the shade implies that the knight's quest will end in death when he tells him to ride "Down the valley of the Shadow" (21), words that refer to death as found in Psalm 23:4: "Though I walk through the valley of the shadow of death."

The word "If" (24), an ambiguous term, makes it possible to read the final line in two contradictory ways. Sanderlin points out that it could mean either, "If you seek for Eldorado, ride boldly over the Mountains of the Moon and down the Valley of the Shadow and you will find it," or, "Ride, boldly ride, if you seek for Eldorado. Your gallantry is laudable, but in the end you will merely continue your search beyond the grave, becoming another pilgrim shade like me" (191). While Sanderlin leaves the poem's meaning open-ended, Silverman insists that the poem concludes on a dismal note: "For the knight's fate is inglorious, a long journey nowhere, overtaken by the failing strength and awareness of aging that weigh on all of Poe's poems in this period" (*Edgar A. Poe*, 403). The vague ending is typical of Poe's writings, for the author often raises contrary possibilities without providing any answers.

Although a puzzling poem, Stovall regards it as "perfectly unified in mood, meaning and form, and is perhaps the most impressive of the short poems of Poe's last period" (225).

"The Raven" (1845)

Poe's most famous poem tells the story of a sorrowful lover of the beautiful, dead Lenore who looks at old books and nearly falls asleep one dreary midnight in December. Suddenly, he hears a tapping at his chamber door. Although filled with fear, he tells himself that some visitor has come and opens the door. When no one appears, he imagines that Lenore may have knocked and whispers her name, hearing only an echo murmuring back. Returning to his chamber, he once again hears the tapping, this time louder. Assuming it is the wind rattling his door, he opens a shutter, and a stately raven steps into his chamber and perches on the bust of Pallas above his chamber door. When he asks its name, the raven replies, "Nevermore." The lonely poet thinks that the raven, like his other friends, will soon leave, but the raven says, "Nevermore." The poet now assumes that this is the one sound the Raven can make.

After he pulls up a cushion in front of the Raven, he is reminded that lost Lenore will never again touch it. Now he thinks the bird has been sent by God to give him some relief from his agony, but the raven once again says, "Nevermore." He pleads with the bird, whom he addresses as "prophet," "bird or devil" (85), to tell him if there is any cure for his distress; the raven croaks, "Nevermore." Still seeing the raven as possibly a devil, the lover asks if he will ever again embrace Lenore in some distant Eden. The answer is the same: "Nevermore." With these words, the narrator orders the raven to return either to the storm or to hell, and to "Take thy beak from out my heart, and take thy form from off my door!" (101). But the raven replies, "Nevermore." As the bird continues to sit on the bust of Pallas with its demonic eyes and its shadow on the floor, the grief-stricken lover realizes that his soul will lie in that shadow forever.

The mood of this poem is sadness, and "the action shows how this mood, as felt by the bereaved lover, shifts from a cherished hope that he will be reunited with his beloved Lenore in some future life to the conviction that he will not" (Stovall, 226). It is divided into two main

THE LINE, "QUOTH THE RAVEN, NEVERMORE" IS ONE OF THE MOST
WELL-KNOWN IN ALL POETRY.

parts, the action before the raven enters and the action after it comes into the chamber. Caputi points out that the first seven stanzas "create the atmosphere of desolation, a desolation which is primarily spiritual, but which also vaguely includes everything beyond the door past which the speaker cannot see" (174).

In these opening verses, the words "nothing more" help evoke the sense of despondency. From stanza eight to the end, the word "Nevermore" is used by the raven as it replies to the lover's questions, which begin lightheartedly, become more serious as the lover is influenced by the somber bird, and finally become words of terror and despair. The seventeenth stanza is the climax of the action, as the lover no longer appeals to the bird, but defies it: "'Be that word our sign of parting, bird or fiend!' I shrieked, upstarting—/ 'Get thee back into the tempest and the Night's Plutonian shore!'" (97–98). The last verse ends with the lover's feeling of total despondency, "'And my soul from out that shadow that lies floating on the floor / Shall be lifted—nevermore!'" (107–108).

Poe carefully designed "The Raven," describing its creation in "The Philosophy of Composition." He says that "the work proceeded step by step, to its completion, with the precision and rigid consequence of a mathematical problem" (979) as he looked at all the elements he considered essential to making an excellent work of art.

To achieve the single effect of sadness, he made the poem brief enough to be read at one sitting. Then he looked at the type of refrain he would use, "some pivot upon which the whole structure might turn" (981). Deciding that a single word to close each stanza would serve "as the best *refrain*" (982), he chose "nevermore" because he determined that "the long *o* [was] the most sonorous vowel in connection with *r* as the most producible consonant" (982). Next turning his attention to finding a "plausible reason for its continuous repetition" (982), he thinks of using "a *non*-reasoning creature capable of speech" (982), a raven. Poe got the effect he desired from the poem by varying the application of the word "Nevermore" as the sorrowful lover questions the raven. He explained, "I saw that I could make the first query . . . a commonplace one, the second less so, the third still less, and so on, until at length the lover, started from his original *nonchalance* by the melancholy character of the word itself, by its frequent repetition, and by a consideration of the ominous reputation of the fowl that uttered it, is at length excited to superstition, and wildly propounds queries of a far different character" (983) to reflect his "intolerable sorrow" (983). This culminates in the last question answered with "Nevermore," which "should involve the utmost conceivable amount of sorrow and despair" (983).

Now ready to write, Poe settled on the poetic techniques he would use. The rhythm is made up of trochees, an accented syllable followed by an unaccented one. Since this is not the pattern of everyday speech, Poe creates a solemn mood by using this foot. Each stanza consists of six long lines, with lines one and three written with eight trochees; lines two, four, and five with seven and a half; and the final line with three and a half. Although these poetic techniques have clearly resonated with millions of readers, not everyone is enthusiastic about Poe's choice of techniques. Writing in 2003, Richard Godden criticized the form of the poem by declaring that "The Raven" "would be eminently readable, were it not that its remorseless trochaic rhythm, extended through one hundred and eight predominantly eight-foot lines, displaces attention from meaning" (997).

Finally, Poe decided on "the mode of bringing together the lover and the Raven" (984). Instead of using a natural setting such as a forest, he set the action in the lover's chamber where memories of the dead Lenore linger.

Poe uses three main symbols to suggest underlying meanings. The primary symbol is the raven, a bird that ancient Greeks regarded both as a prophet, being sacred to their god Apollo, and a foreteller of death because droves of ravens arrived on battlefields after a war to scavenge for dead bodies (Thompson, *Selected Writings*, 59n5). For Poe, the raven is "emblematical of *Mournful and never ending Remembrance*" ("The Philosophy of Composition," 987). Therefore, this bird stands for memory, showing that the sorrowful lover will always remain bereaved because he will always remember Lenore. A second symbol is the "bust of Pallas." Buranelli explains that this statue, besides standing for the Greek goddess of wisdom, "also represents the life of learning into which the narrator of the poem has plunged in order to drown his sorrow" (102). The silent, white bust is contrasted with the croaking, black bird, "one symbolizing serene wisdom and the other crushing fate" (Buranelli, 102). The raven's word, "Nevermore," is also a symbol. As it is repeated over and over again, it, according to Buranelli, "begins to take on overtones of universal tragedy, reminding the reader that the tramp of death can be heard by us all, and not just by one individual asking about one dead woman" (102).

Literary Reception

Poe's first volumes of verse were little noticed and scarcely praised. His 1829 poems were called "nonsense, rather exquisite nonsense" (Neal, 3), and the works in his 1831 *Poems* were described as "a strange mixture of genius and nonsense" (quoted in Carlson, *Critical Essays*, 1).

However, Poe received national and international fame in January 1845 with the publication of "The Raven." The poem was an immediate hit, received in a way that "might be compared to that of some uproariously successful hit song today" (Silverman, *Edgar A. Poe*, 237).

Readers agreed with the publisher that it is "unsurpassed in English poetry for subtle conception, masterly ingenuity of versification, and consistent, sustaining of imaginative lift. . . . It will stick to the memory of everybody who reads it" (quoted in Ingram, 219–220). During the first weeks of 1845, it was repeatedly published in magazines and newspapers. From 1845 to 1849, it was reprinted extensively in America and Europe. The English poet Elizabeth Barrett [Browning] was most impressed with it, writing to Poe, "This vivid writing!—this power *which* is felt! 'The Raven' has produced a sensation—a 'fit horror,' here in England. Some of my friends are taken by the fear of it and some by the music. I hear of persons *haunted* by the Nevermore, and one acquaintance of mine, who has the misfortune of possessing a 'bust of Pallas,' never can bear to look at it in the twilight" (quoted in Ingram, 221). It was so popular that authors parodied it with such pieces as "The Owl," "The Craven," and "The Turkey" (Thompson, *Selected Writings*, 57).

After Poe became a famous poet with the publication of the "The Raven," more critics examined his poetry. A few Americans thought he was a good poet, praising his poems for possessing "a pure and original vein" (Lowell, 16) and commending them for being "constructed with wonderful ingenuity, and finished with consummate art" (Griswold, "Memoir," 55). However, most viewed him as no more than mediocre, complaining that his poems "leave us something to desire or demand" (Fuller, "Review of *The Raven*," 39). One of the most disapproving was Ralph Waldo Emerson who, seeing only frivolity in Poe's verse forms, dismissed him as "*the jingle-man*" (quoted in Howells, 67).

In the second half of the nineteenth century, most American writers and critics did not like Poe's poetry any better than his prose. For example, Henry James condemned his poetry as "very valueless verses" (65), and

Walt Whitman faulted them for having "no heat," even though they were "imaginative," "brilliant and dazzling" (83). In spite of the negative critical evaluation, Poe's poetry, particularly "The Raven," continued to be popular. Poe's first scholarly biographer, John Henry Ingram, declared in 1880 that "The Raven" has "done more for the renown of American letters than any other single work," quickly spreading "over the whole of the United States, calling into existence parodies and imitations innumerable, and, indeed, creating quite a literature of its own; it carried its author's name and fame from shore to shore, inducing veritable poets in other lands . . . to attempt to transmute its magical charms into their tongues; it drew admiring testimony from some of the finest spirits of the age" (221).

Many Europeans poets admired Poe. The famous nineteenth century English poet Algernon Charles Swinburne thought Poe was a "strong and delicate genius" (79). The French were especially impressed with Poe. In 1857, French poet Charles Baudelaire censured Americans for not appreciating this "great" man who had "noble conceptions" and was able to understand "the natural perversity of man" (65–66). The poet Mallarmé expressed similar views, describing Poe as "one of the most marvelous minds the world has ever known" (quoted in P. F. Quinn, 4).

Although by the twentieth century "The Raven" was even more popular with the general public, and had been translated into numerous languages, including German, French, Hungarian, Latin, Dutch, and Portuguese (Richards, 205), Poe was still not universally admired. U.S. writers said little about him, while in England the response remained mixed. A few regarded Poe as the greatest U.S. poet, who "constantly and inevitably produced magic where his greatest contemporaries produced only beauty" (Shaw, 88), but others maintained that he was not a major poet and that his poetry was ruined by "shades of vulgarity" (Huxley, 160–161). T. S. Eliot found Poe's "immense" influence on French poets "puzzling" because he thought Poe's ideas were unsophisticated and his diction faulty (205, 209–210). Even "The Raven" was dismissed by Irish poet William Butler Yeats as an "insincere and vulgar" poem, having no "permanent literary value of any kind" because "its subject is a commonplace and its execution a rhythmical trick. Its rhythm never lives for a moment, never once moves with an emotional life" (77).

Since World War II, Poe has slowly gained greater critical acceptance as a poet, but his greatness is still often questioned. Although many critics no longer agree with Emerson that Poe is merely a "jingle-man," he is not considered one of the great American writers even though he wrote the most popular American poem, "The Raven." Silverman explains that "for many of the most discriminating critics, Poe succeeded all too well in suiting the popular taste, producing a work fatally destined to be Beloved, a poem for people who don't like poetry" (*Edgar A. Poe*, 239).

In spite of the critics, Poe's popularity with readers has continued unabated to this day. In high school and college English classrooms, Poe's poetry is almost always found in anthologies of American literature and of poetry. So, although Poe's poetry is not greatly admired by the critics, it is loved by the masses.

Chapter 5

Poe's Place in Literature

CRITICS HAVE BEEN WIDELY DIVIDED on Poe's achievements as a writer. According to Vincent Buranelli, "Quotations can be accumulated to prove that Poe is a second-rate hack—or a creative genius who falls just short of the supreme masters. He is repeatedly called overrated, and underrated. In an amazing international clash of opinion, Americans marvel at the high place that Poe holds in France, while Frenchmen shake their heads over the dim-wittedness of Americans who do not appreciate the magisterial literary personality they have given to the world" (128).

During Poe's lifetime, people both loved and despised his writings. Best known as a magazine editor and a harsh literary critic, he was also recognized for his short stories and poems. Generally, his tales were praised, and one, "The Gold-Bug," was very successful. Poe claimed that this tale "circulated to a greater extent than any American tale, before or since" (quoted in Silverman, *New Essays*, 8). He saw it translated into French and made into a play during his lifetime. Even more popular was "The Raven," which brought Poe international recognition.

Immediately after his death, Poe's reputation in America fell immensely because of Griswold's character assassination in his biography of Poe. Commentators, who now saw Poe as a degenerate drug addict and alcoholic, failed to separate the works from the man, and, as a result, looked upon Poe's protagonists as "vulgarly Gothic and Decadent" men who, like the author, lacked "humanity" and "heart" (Carlson, *Recognition*, ix).

Accordingly, Poe was treated as a minor writer who did not deserve the respect of mature adults, an idea Henry James made clear in 1876 when he asserted, "An enthusiasm for Poe is the mark of a decidedly primitive stage of reflection" (66).

After World War I, scholars took a renewed interest in Poe and his writings, and an impressive body of scholarship appeared. Stanford English professor Yvor Winters, who seriously disliked Poe, became greatly alarmed, fearing that critics were trying to promote Poe as a writer of first rank. In 1937, he blasted Poe as "a bad writer accidentally and temporarily popular" (177). Scholar F. O. Matthiessen evidently agreed with Winters's negative view, for he omitted Poe in his monumental and influential study of nineteenth century American literature, *American Renaissance*, first published in 1941. As a result, Poe was kept out of the mainstream of major Romantic authors for decades. He was seen as a minor author who lacked depth, as poet T. S. Eliot, lecturing in 1948, declared. Although Eliot granted that Poe "had a powerful intellect," it was only "the intellect of a highly gifted young person before puberty" (212).

Across the ocean in Europe, however, Poe achieved great critical acclaim in the hundred years after his death. Baudelaire, Fyodor Dostoyevsky, Sigmund Freud, Thomas Mann, and D. H. Lawrence "all saw in Poe's tales a profound delineation of the disintegrated modern psyche" (Silverman, *New Essays*, 15), and they greatly admired his works.

Since World War II, American scholars have begun to regard Poe as a major American writer, famous for his unnerving tales of horror, clever detective stories, and poignant poems. Scholarly journals are filled with articles examining Poe's works, and books have been written about them. Carlson explains that "the great postwar efflorescence of existentialism in literature, with its exploitation of the irrational, the grotesque, the fantastic, the psychotic, and the sadistic, has brought to many readers of Poe the 'shock of recognition': the discovery of Poe as a great forerunner exploring the real horrors and self-realizations of modern man" (*Recognition*, xi). In addition to critical analyses of Poe's works, scholars have also begun to reevaluate his life. A number of biographies have appeared in the last few decades; of greatest importance are Kenneth Silverman's *Edgar A. Poe: Mournful and Never-ending Remembrance*, published in 1991, and Arthur Hobson Quinn's *Edgar Allan Poe: A Critical Biography*, (first published in 1941), reissued in 1998.

Even though Poe has received little scholarly acclaim, the reading public never lost interest in his tales and poems. His works have constantly been in print, and they have been translated into a variety of languages. The Edgar Allan Poe Society of Baltimore claims that "first printings of Poe's books sell for thousands, his manuscripts for tens of thousands. His 1827 *Tamerlane and Minor Poems* is one of the most valuable books ever printed in the United States" ("Poe's Enduring Fame").

Poe has had a huge influence on writers, composers, and filmmakers. He invented "one of the most popular literary entertainments ever conceived, the tale of crime and detection. Many of the devices he introduced remain conventions of the genre even today—the detective's sidekick, the investigation of material clues, the locked-room mystery" (Silverman, *New Essays*, 8). Poe's Dupin forms the model for detectives found in literature, including Sir Arthur Conan Doyle's Sherlock Holmes, and in television shows, such as *Columbo* and *Monk*. Besides paving the way for modern literary detective stories, Poe's new genre, as professor John T. Irwin contends, "produced the dominant modern genre . . . the genre of an age dominated by science and technology, an age characterized by mental-work-as-analysis" (xvi). Irwin writes that psychoanalysts, literary critics, physicists, and diagnosticians all follow Dupin's methods: "the patient amassing of clues, the false leads, the painstaking analysis, and ultimate triumph" (xvii).

In fiction, Edgar Allan Poe appears as a character in numerous books. For example, he is a visitor to Paris who meets and helps Charles Baudelaire in Barry Perowne's *A Singular Conspiracy* (1974); an investigator in Avi's juvenile novel, *The Man Who Was Poe* (1989); an explorer of the inhabited center of the world in Rudy Rucker's *The Hollow Earth* (1990); a man whose mysterious death is investigated by C. Auguste Dupin in George Egon Hatvary's *The Murder of Edgar Allan Poe: A Novel* (1997); a schoolboy in England in Andrew Taylor's historical mystery novel, *An Unpardonable Crime* (2003); and himself in Matthew Pearl's *The Poe Shadow* (2006), a novel which reexamines the unusual events of Poe's death.

His works are also used by authors. For instance, Harold Schechter has written a series of historical and mystery novels with titles that mimic Poe's words: *Nevermore: A Novel* (1999), *The Hum Bug: A Novel* (2001), *The Mask of Red Death: An Edgar Allan Poe Mystery* (2004), and *The Tell-Tale Corpse: An Edgar Allan Poe Mystery* (2006). Poe's works are also referenced by writers. For example, Vladimirovich Nabokov's *Lolita* (1955) includes a character named Annabel Leigh who is just like Poe's maiden; Joan Aiken's novel *Arabel's Raven* (1974) features a pet raven named Mortimer who says "Nevermore"; Stephen King compares an omen to Poe's raven in *Insomnia* (1994); King and Peter Straub title the third section of *Black House* (2001) "Night's Plutonian Shore" and include a talking crow.

In music, Poe's works and life have inspired composers, singers, and instrumentalists for more than one hundred years. Classical musicians in various countries have used Poe's works as the basis for their compositions, including such prominent composers as Claude Debussy, writing the unfinished operas "The Fall of the House of Usher" and "The Devil in the Belfry," and Sergei Rachmaninoff, composing a choral symphony of "The Bells." Popular musicians working in various genres—country, blues, folk, rap, pop, modern rock, and heavy metal—have also been influenced by Poe. Artists and bands that have recorded songs inspired by Poe include Britney Spears, Bob Dylan, Joan Baez, Lou Reed, the Alan Parsons Project, the Smithereens, Green Day, Good Charlotte, Cradle of Filth, Utada Hikaru, Iron Maiden, and Insane Clown Posse.

Poe has also done well in Hollywood. Shawn James Rosenheim claims that "more film adaptations have been made of Poe's work than of any other American writer, ranging from drive-in horror movies to a striking association between Poe and the cinematic avant-garde" (116). During the 1960s, director Roger Corman and actor Vincent Price made Poe into a household word by filming a series of movies on Poe's tales and his poem "The Raven." Poe's short stories and poems have been produced in black and white and in color; as silent films and as sound films; as animated films and as films with live action. In addition to productions made of Poe's works, there have been a number of films about his life and his genres.

So popular is Poe in American culture that he has become an icon. Parodies of his works are found on television shows such as *The Simpsons*, *Garfield and Friends*, *The Addams Family*, *The Munsters*, and *Sabrina, the Teenage Witch*. Images of Poe are found on coffee mugs, T-shirts, bookmarks, and postcards. Athletes have taken their names from Poe's works, including the NFL team the Baltimore Ravens and professional wrestler Raven, whose real name is Scott Levy. A musician and writer born Annabel McMullin now goes by the name of Annabel Lee.

POE'S WORK HAS BEEN THE SOURCE OF BOOKS, CARTOONS, AND EVEN
MOVIES. IN THIS SCENE FROM THE 1935 VERSION OF *THE RAVEN*,
BELA LUGOSI LISTENS TO THE FAMOUS BIRD.

The most prestigious honor society at the University of Virginia, where Poe attended college, is called "The Raven Society."

Arthur Hobson Quinn is correct when he says that Poe's "fame is now secure. The America in which he could find no adequate reward treasures every word he wrote, and in every city in which he lived, except the city of his birth, stands a lasting memorial to him. He has become a world artist and through the translations of his writings he speaks today to every civilized country" (695). The public continues to read Poe's works, and scholars keep studying them because he appeals to a variety of readers. He is read and understood by inexperienced readers who love a good mystery, a thrilling adventure, or a scary horror story; he is also appreciated by more sophisticated readers who explore their own beliefs and experiences as they read his works.

Poe is now seen as one of America's greatest writers. He is "not only the one American, but also the one writer in the English language, who was at once foremost in criticism, supreme in fiction, and in poetry destined to be immortal" (A. H. Quinn, 695). Poe's fame comes not only because of his excellent writings but also because of his broad influence. Buranelli maintains that if a complete survey were made of Poe's influence on writers, artists, popular culture, and readers, "Poe would be revealed for what he is—America's greatest writer, and the American writer of greatest significance in world literature" (133).

Works

Collections in Books

1827   *Tamerlane and Other Poems*
1829   *Al Aaraaf, Tamerlane, and Minor Poems*
1831   *Poems by Edgar A. Poe . . . Second Edition*
1839   *The Conchologist's First Book* [By Thomas Wyatt]
        Tales of the Grotesque and Arabesque
1843   *The Prose Romances of Edgar A. Poe*
1845   *Tales*
        The Raven and Other Poems
1849, 1855   *The Works of Edgar Allan Poe*

Poems

1827   "Tamerlane"
        Song, I saw thee on thy bridal day
        "Dreams"
        "Visit of the Dead" (renamed "Spirits of the Dead")
        "Evening Star"
        "Imitation" (renamed "A Dream within a Dream")
        Stanzas, In youth have I known one with whom the Earth
        Poem, without title (renamed "A Dream")
        Poem, without title (renamed "The Happiest Day, The Happiest Hour)"
        "The Lake: To ____"
1829   Poem, without title (renamed "Sonnet—to Science")

"Al Aaraaf"
"Romance"
To____, The bowers whereat, in dreams, I see
"To the River____"
To____, I heed not that my earthly lot
"Fairy-Land"
1831   "To Helen"
"Israfel"
"The Doomed City" (renamed "The City in the Sea")
"Irene" (renamed "The Sleeper")
"A Pæan" (renamed "Lenore")
"The Valley Nis" (renamed "The Valley of Unrest")
1833   "The Coliseum"
1834   "To One in Paradise"
1835   "Hymn"
"To F___" (renamed "To Mary"; renamed "To One Departed")
"To F___s. S. O___d" (renamed "Lines Written in an Album")
"Scenes from 'Politian'" (1835–36, 1923)
1837   "Ballad" (renamed "Bridal Ballad")
"Sonnet—To Zante"
1839   "The Haunted Palace"
1840   "Silence. A Sonnet" (renamed "Sonnet—Silence")
1843   "The Conqueror Worm"
1844   "Dream-Land"
1845   "The Raven"
"Eulalie—A Song"
1846   "To Her Whose Name is Written Below" (renamed "A Valentine")
1847   "To M. L. S___"
"Ulalume—A Ballad"
1848   "Sonnet" (renamed "An Enigma")

*To*____, Not long ago, the writer of these lines
*To*____, I saw thee once (renamed "To Helen")
1849   "Eldorado"
       "For Annie"
       "Sonnet—To My Mother"
       "Annabel Lee," posthumously
       "The Bells," posthumously
Uncollected   "Elizabeth"
             "Serenade"

Tales

1832   "Metzengerstein"
       "The Duc de L'Omelette"
       "A Tale of Jerusalem"
       "A Decided Loss" (renamed "Loss of Breath")
       "The Bargain Lost" (renamed "Bon Bon")
1833   "MS. Found in a Bottle"
1834   "The Assignation"
1835   "Berenice"
       "Morella—A Tale"
       "Lionizing"
       "Hans Phaall—A Tale"
       "King Pest the First. A Tale Containing an
          Allegory"
       "Shadow. A Fable" (renamed "Shadow—A
          Parable")
1836   "Epimanes" (renamed "Four Beasts in One—
          the Homo-Cameleopard)
1837   "Von Jung, the Mystic" (renamed
          "Mystification")
1838   "Siope—A Fable" (renamed "Silence—
          A Fable")
       "Ligeia"
       "Psyche Zenobia" (renamed "How to Write a
          Blackwood Article")
       "The Scythe of Time" (renamed "A
          Predicament")

1839   "The Devil in the Belfry"
        "The Man That was Used Up. A Tale of the
           Late Bugaboo and Kickapoo Campaign"
        "The Fall of the House of Usher"
        "William Wilson"
        "The Conversation of Eiros and Charmion"
1840   "Why the Little Frenchman Wears His Hand in
           a Sling"
        "Peter Pendulum, The Business Man" (renamed
           "The Business Man")
        "The Philosophy of Furniture"
        "The Man of the Crowd"
1841   "The Murders in the Rue Morgue"
        "A Descent into the Maelström"
        "The Island of the Fay"
        "The Colloquy of Monos and Una"
        "Never Bet Your Head" (renamed "Never Bet
           the Devil Your Head")
        "Eleonora"
        "A Succession of Sundays" (renamed "Three
           Sundays in a Week")
1842   "Life in Death" (renamed "The Oval Portrait")
        "The Mask of the Red Death" (renamed "The
           Masque of the Red Death")
        "The Landscape Garden"
        "The Mystery of Marie Rogêt" (1842–1843)
        "The Pit and the Pendulum"
1843   "The Tell-Tale Heart"
        "The Gold-Bug"
        "The Black Cat"
        "Raising the Wind; or, Diddling Considered as
           One of the Exact Sciences"
1844   "Morning on the Wissahiccon"
        "The Spectacles"
        "A Tale of the Ragged Mountains"
        "The Balloon Hoax"

"The Premature Burial"
"Mesmeric Revelation"
"The Oblong Box"
"The Angel of the Odd—An Extravaganza"
"Thou Art the Man"
"The Literary Life of Thingum Bob"
"The Purloined Letter"
1845   "The Thousand-and-Second Tale of Scheherazade"
"Some Words with a Mummy"
"The Power of Words"
"The Imp of the Perverse"
"The System of Dr. Tarr and Prof. Fether"
"The Facts in the Case of M. Valdemar"
1846   "The Sphinx"
"The Cask of Amontillado"
1847   "The Domain of Arnheim"
1849   "Mellonta Tauta"
"Hop-Frog, or The Eight Chained Orang-Outangs"
"Von Kempelen and His Discovery"
"X-ing a Paragrab"
"Landor's Cottage"

Long Prose Works

1838   *The Narrative of Arthur Gordon Pym*, a novel
1840   *The Journal of Julius Rodman* (incomplete and not published in book form)
1848   *Eureka: A Prose Poem*

Criticism

1831   "Letter to B_____"
1836   Critique of *The Culprit Fay and Other Poems* by Joseph Rodman Drake and *Alnwick Castle, with Other Poems* by Fitz-Greene Halleck

1837   Critique of *Poems* by William Cullen Bryant
1841   Critique of *The Old Curiosity Shop, and Other Tales* and *Master Humphrey's Clock* by Charles Dickens
        Critique of *The Quacks of Helicon: A Satire* by L. A. Wilmer
1842   "Exordium"
        Critique of *Ballads and Other Poems* by Henry Wadsworth Longfellow
        Critique of *Twice-Told Tales* by Nathaniel Hawthorne
1845   "The American Drama"
        "Preface" to *The Raven and Other Poems*
        "Marginalia" (1845–1849)
1846   "The Philosophy of Composition"
1848   "The Rationale of Verse" (first printed in 1843 as "Notes on English Verse")
1850   "The Poetic Principle"

Filmography

Many of Poe's works have been made into films. Below is a list of the more recent versions that are available on DVD or VHS.

"The Black Cat." *Masters of Horror*, TV series. Dir. Stuart Gordon. IDT Entertainment. 2007.

The Cask of Amontillado. Film. Dir. Mario Cavalli. Pizzazz Pictures. 1998.

The House of Usher. Film. Dir. Alan Birkinshaw. Breton Film Productions. 1988.

The Masque of the Red Death. Film. Dir. Larry Brand. Concorde Pictures. 1989.

The Murders in the Rue Morgue. TV movie. Dir. Jeannot Szwarc. International Film Productions. 1986.

The Pit and the Pendulum. Independent film. Dir. Stuart Gordon. Empire Pictures. 1991.

The Raven. Film short. *The Raven. . . Nevermore*. Dir. Tinieblas González. Tinieblas Films. 1999.

The Raven. Short film with puppets. Dir. Peter Bradley. 2003.

The Tell-Tale Heart. Animated film. Dir. Ted Parmelee. UPA. 1953.

The Tell-Tale Heart. Film. Dir. Scott Mansfield. Monterey Video. 2000.

The Tell-Tale-Heart. Computer-animated short. Created by Michael Swertfager. Alpha Dog Creations. 2007.

Other Films on Poe and His Works
The Death of Poe. Film. Dir. Mark Redfield. Redfield Arts. 2006.

The Edgar Allan Poe Collection. Vol. 1. Dir. George Higham, Peter Bradley, and Alfonso Suarez. Lurker Films, Inc. 2005. Contains "Annabel Lee," "The Raven," and "The Tell-Tale Heart."

Nevermore: The Nightmares of Edgar Allan Poe. Film. Dir. Ric White. 2005. Contains "The Premature Burial," "The Tell-Tale Heart," "The Cask of Amontillado," and "The Raven."

Poe. Short Black-and-white Film. Dir. Gregory Nixon. 2000.

Chronology

1809
Edgar Poe born in Boston on January 19 to Elizabeth and David Poe.

1811
Poe's father disappears; Poe's mother dies of consumption. Poe becomes ward of John and Frances Allan of Richmond, Virginia.

1815–1820
The Allans move to London; Poe attends boarding school in England.

1820
The Allans return to Richmond; Poe enters Richmond Academy.

1822
Virginia Eliza Clemm, Poe's future wife, born in Baltimore on August 15.

1825
John Allan inherits his uncle's fortune.
Poe becomes engaged to Sarah Elmira Royster.

1826
Poe attends University of Virginia for one year.

1827
Poe returns to Richmond; fights with Allan; enlists in the
U.S. Army.
Tamerlane and Other Poems published.

1829
Mrs. Frances Allan dies on February 28.
Poe leaves the army.
Al Aaraaf, Tamerlane, and Minor Poems published.

1830
Poe enters U.S. Military Academy at West Point.
John Allan remarries in October.

1831
Poe court-martialed from West Point; moves to Baltimore
and lives with his aunt Maria Clemm, his grandmother,
his brother Henry and his cousins Virginia and Henry.
Poems by Edgar A. Poe . . . Second Edition published.

1832
First short stories published: "Metzengertein," "The Duc
de L'Omelette," "A Tale of Jerusalem," "A Decided Loss"
("Loss of Breath"), and "The Bargain Lost" ("Bon-Bon").

1833
Poe wins $50 prize for "MS. Found in a Bottle."

1834
John Allan dies on March 27 and leaves Poe no inheritance.

1835
Poe accepts editor job with *The Southern Literary Messen-
ger*; moves to Richmond.
Grandmother Elizabeth Cairnes Poe dies.

1836
Poe marries Virginia Clemm on May 16; writes many critical reviews.

1837
Poe leaves *The Southern Literary Messenger*; moves to New York with his family but cannot find work.

1838
Poe moves his family to Philadelphia.
The Narrative of Arthur Gordon Pym and "Ligeia" published.

1839
Poe becomes coeditor of *Burton's Gentleman's Magazine*. "The Fall of the House of Usher," "William Wilson," and *Tales of the Grotesque and Arabesque*, Poe's first volume of stories, published.

1840
Poe leaves *Burton's Gentleman's*; plans his own journal.

1841
Poe takes job as editor of *Graham's Magazine*.
"The Murders in the Rue Morgue" published.

1842
Virginia becomes sick with tuberculosis.
Poe resigns from *Graham's*.
"The Mask [later spelled "Masque"] of the Red Death," "The Pit and the Pendulum," "The Mystery of Marie Rogêt," and other tales published.

1843
Poe revives plans for magazine renamed *Stylus*; wins $100 prize for "The Gold-Bug."

"The Tell-Tale Heart," "The Black Cat," and other tales also published.

1844

Poe moves with family to New York City; joins staff of the New York *Mirror*.
"The Balloon Hoax," "The Premature Burial," "The Purloined Letter," and other tales published.

1845

Poe is coeditor and for a few months owner of *The Broadway Journal*; lectures on poetry.
"The Raven," *The Raven and Other Poems*, and tales published.

1846

Poe stops publication of *The Broadway Journal*; moves to Fordham (near New York City).
"The Cask of Amontillado" published.

1847

Virginia dies on January 30.
"Ulalume" published.

1848

Poe professes love for Mrs. Annie Richmond; becomes engaged to Sarah Helen Whitman; gives lectures.
"The Poetic Principle" and "Eureka" published.

1849

Poe receives proposal to publish the *Stylus* in Illinois; becomes engaged to Elmira Royster Shelton of Richmond. Poe dies in Baltimore on October 7.
"Eldorado" published; "Annabel Lee" and "The Bells" published posthumously.

Notes

Chapter 1

p. 12, par.1, Poe thought that his father stayed with his mother and died about the same time she did. Writing to Judge Beverly Tucker of Virginia on December 1, 1835, Poe stated, "Both died (as you may remember) within a few weeks of each other." The judge did not contradict him. John Ward Ostrom, ed., *The Letters of Edgar Allan Poe*, Vol. 1 (New York: Gordian Press, Inc., 1966), 78–79. Poe's first major biographer, John H. Ingram, writing in 1880, also believed that David Poe remained with his family and was with them when they moved to Richmond, Virginia, where "early in 1811, David Poe died of consumption." *Edgar Allan Poe: His Life, Letters, and Opinions* (New York: AMS Press, Inc., 1965), 6. This same thought was repeated in an article published in March 1904 in *The Century*: "David Poe, the father, died of consumption late in the spring of 1811, while the family was living in Norfolk. . . . David Poe was buried in one of the cemeteries of Norfolk." Charles Marshall Graves, "Landmarks of Poe in Richmond," in *The Edgar Allan Poe Scrapbook*, ed. Peter Haining (New York: Schocken Books, 1978), 34.

p. 12, par. 2, For an analysis of the effects of Elizabeth Arnold Poe's death on her son, *see* Phillip L. Roderick, *The Fall of the House of Poe and Other Essays* (New York: iUniverse, 2006), 1–50.

p. 18, par. 1, One of Poe's contemporaries at the University of Virginia, T. G. Tucker, wrote a report of his remembrances of Poe, which was published in the *University of Virginia Magazine* in 1880. He said that Poe often entertained him "by reading to him the early productions of his youth—productions that his critical hand afterwards destroyed, thinking them unfit for publication. Sometimes, when he had written an article that Tucker would especially praise, he would call in a few of his friends and read it to them. Those men who were fortunate enough to hear these impromptu readings never forgot them, and those of the number who were still living in 1880 declared that there was no impression on their minds more strikingly vivid." T. G. Tucker, "The University Story-teller," in Haining, *The Edgar Allan Poe Scrapbook*, 39–40.

p. 43, par. 2, The newspapers of the time made wild conjectures about the cause of Poe's death. One stated that Poe was robbed and left in a gutter; another related that the poet was found in Lexington Market, lying on barrels and covered with flies; a third said that the former West Pointer met with West Point cadets who lured him into some secret government operations; still another newspaper attributed Poe's death to over imbibing in alcohol at a birthday party; one declared that the writer had committed suicide; several stated that he had died of brain congestion or cerebral inflammation. *See* Matthew Pearl, *The Poe Shadow* (New York: Random House, 2006), 181; and Kenneth Silverman, *Edgar A. Poe: Mournful and Neverending Remembrance* (New York: HarperCollins, 1991), 435.

p. 43, par. 2, The theory that Poe died of alcohol-related problems has been advanced in Matthew Pearl's novel *The Poe Shadow* in which Pearl carefully researched details about Poe's last days and his death. According to Pearl, Poe's death probably took place in this way:

After leaving Richmond to go to New York to make arrangements for Muddy to come to Virginia to live with him and his fiancée, he stopped in Baltimore to visit and stay with N. C. Brooks, an editor and publisher, to try to raise money for his new magazine, *Stylus*. However, Brooks' home was either burning or had just burned down, depending on what date Poe actually arrived (Pearl, 366). Since Poe now needed to rent a hotel room, an expense the poor man could ill afford, he did not stay long in Baltimore but quickly left for Philadelphia where he planned to edit a book of poems, a task he intended to do, for he wrote to his mother-in-law: "Mr. Loud, the husband of Mrs. St. Leon Loud, the poetess of Philadelphia, called on me the other day and offered me $100 to edit his wife's poems. Of course, I accepted the offer. The whole labor will not occupy me three days" (*Letters*, Vol. 2, 458–459). Pearl also points out that Poe expected to go to Philadelphia at this time because he had written to Muddy telling her to "write immediately to Phil[adelphia] so that your letter will be there when I arrive." He also directed her to address the letter to "E. S. T. Grey Esq" "For fear I should not get the letter" (*Letters*, Vol. 2, 461), probably because any letter addressed to "E. A. Poe" would be immediately forwarded to New York. According to the Philadelphia Public Ledger, on October 3, a letter addressed to "E. S. F. Grey" was waiting at the post office for pickup (Pearl, 343–344). (Either Muddy or the postmaster probably thought the "T" was an "F.") However, this letter was never picked up.

Pearl imagines that Poe was on a train headed for Philadelphia when he met an old friend, possibly Z. Collins Lee, a college classmate and district attorney who attended Poe's funeral. Invited to have a drink, Poe amiably took one. But, unfortunately for the poet, who was sensitive to alcohol, he became sick after his friend left him. Appearing intoxicated, Poe, Pearl suggests, was removed from the train by the conductor and sent back to Baltimore.

Incapacitated in Baltimore, Pearl thinks Poe became soaked in a rainstorm and exchanged his drenched clothes for dry ones that did not fit well, a fairly common practice at the time. Needing to find shelter, Poe went to a nearby hotel and tavern, which, on October 3, was also a polling station for an election, where he was found by Walker. The rest of Pearl's story follows the known facts of Poe's death.

p. 44, par. 1, The intriguing idea that Poe died from rabies was advanced by R. Michael Benitez, M.D., "Rabies," *Maryland Medical Journal*, 45 (September 1996), 765–769.

p. 48, par. 2, In Griswold's "Memoir," "Poe is seen as ungenerous and self-absorbed, a backbiter, a debtor, a criminal, a racist, a drunkard, a drug addict, a misogynist, and even a pedophile" (Thompson, *Selected Writings*; xlv). Although Poe did drink and was often in debt, Griswold exaggerates these faults. His claims that Poe was not a true friend are made-up allegations based on Griswold's forgery of Poe's letters. Griswold's other assertions are also bogus. Poe was not a pedophile. As has been noted by many biographers, even though he married a young teen, probably to keep his family together, he was not interested in other young women.

The charge that Poe was a misogynist seems unlikely based on his strong love for many women, in particular Muddy and Virginia. Furthermore, in recent years, feminists have reevaluated the way he treats women in his stories; the new view is that Poe, instead of possessing "a tremendous hatred and loathing for women, as evidenced by the horrendous treatment and death they inevitable suffer at the hands of either fate, or their male companions," they now see things in an entirely different way

(Roderick, 16, 18). Phillip L. Roderick reviews the works of four feminists—Paul Kot in "Feminist 'Re-Visioning' of the Tale of Women," Cynthia S. Jordan in *Second Stories: The Politics of Language, Form and Gender in Early American Fictions*, Monika Elbert in "Poe's Gothic Mother and the Incubation of Language," and Joan Dayan in "Poe's Women: A Feminist Poe?"—and finds that they all see that Poe is "far more generous toward women in his narratives that [sic] it initially appears. . . . Feminist revisioning has now enabled feminist critics to see that Poe's tendency to first silence, then brutally injure and later kill off his female characters is neither an act of malevolence, nor an indication of Poe's views about women. Instead of the death of the female character representing the final act, critics and readers now realize that in many ways, the female characters ultimately end up triumphant over their male oppressors" (18). For a more complete discussion of this topic, *see* Roderick, 16–20.

The charge that Poe was a racist has received much attention in the last decades. An excellent work on this topic is Terence Whalen, *Poe and the Masses: The Political Economy of Literature in Antebellum America* (Princeton, NJ: Princeton University Press, 1999), 111–140, 293–302. Whalen carefully analyzes older points of view that define Poe as a racist; he clearly and effectively explains why they are wrong; and he concludes that Poe was an average racist for the pre-Civil War days.

Whalen first looks at a book edited by Vincent Freimarck and Bernard Rosenthal. See *Race and the American Romantics* (New York: Schocken Books, 1971). The editors describe Poe as "certainly the most blatant racist among the American Romantics" (3), basing their claim on a racist article they incorrectly attributed to Poe. Whalen then explains that even when Rosenthal found out that the article on which he based his conclusion was written by someone else, he still maintained his mistaken view in an article entitled "Poe, Slavery, and the *Southern Literary Messenger*: A Reexamination," *Poe Studies* 7 (December 1974), 29–38.

Whalen also looks at critics who generalize about Poe, seeing him as a racist primarily because he was a southerner living just before the Civil War. However, they do not offer convincing proof. *See* Kenneth Alan Hovey, "Critical Provincialism: Poe's Poetic Principle in Antebellum Context," *American Quarterly* 39 (Fall 1987), 347, 353n40; A. Robert Lee, "'Impudent and Ingenious Fiction': Poe's *The Narrative of Arthur Gordon Pym of Nantucket*," in *Edgar Allan Poe: The Design of Order* (New York: Barnes and Noble, 1987), 128; John Carlos Rowe, "Poe, Antebellum Slavery, and Modern Criticism," in *Poe's Pym: Critical Explorations*, ed. Richard Kopley (Durham, NC: Duke University Press, 1992), 117; and Craig Werner, "The Insurrection of Subjugated Knowledge: Poe and Ishmael Reed," in *Poe and Our Times: Influences and Affinities*, ed. Benjamin Franklin Fisher IV (Baltimore: The Edgar Allan Poe Society, 1986), 155.

Whalen concludes that Poe was not a blatant racist but one who attempted to hold a type of average racism that would appeal to the majority of the subscribers of his magazines.

Chapter 2

p. 55, par. 2, For a detailed discussion of the American publishing industry during Poe's time, *see* Terence Whalen, "Poe and the American Publishing Industry," in *A Historical Guide to Edgar Allan Poe*, ed. J. Gerald Kennedy (New York: Oxford University Press, 2001), 63–93.

p. 56, par. 1, For a thorough discussion of literary trends, see Walter Blair, et al., *American Literature: A Brief*

History. Revised ed. (Glenview, Il: Scott, Foresman, and Co., 1974), 64–73, 112–137.

Chapter 3

All references to Poe's works come from: Edgar Allan Poe, *The Complete Tales and Poems of Edgar Allan Poe with Selections From His Critical Writings*. Introduction and explanatory notes by Arthur Hobson Quinn. Bibliographical notes by Edward H. O'Neill (New York: Barnes & Noble, 1992).

p. 59, par. 2, A number of critics think that Montresor must be insane. Stuart Levine writes that "'The Cask' has no passage to tell the reader that the narrator is mad: the entire story does that." *Edgar Poe: Seer and Craftsman* (Deland, FL: Everett/Edwards, 1972), 80. Edward Hutchins Davidson agrees: "We never know what has made him hate Fortunato nor are we aware that he has ever laid out any plan to effect his revenge. . . . There is nothing intellectual here; everything is mad and improvisatory." *Poe, A Critical Study* (Cambridge: Harvard University Press, 1957), 201–202. Richard M. Fletcher also finds that Montresor's actions are irrational and demonstrate insanity. *The Stylistic Development of Edgar Allan Poe* (The Hague: Mouton, 1973), 167. And Stephen Peithman argues that "If there is any doubt that Montresor is mad, consider how he echoes Fortunato scream for scream, shrieking even louder than his victim." "The Cask of Amontillado," in *The Annotated Tales of Edgar Allan Poe*, ed. Stephen Peithman (Garden City, NY: Doubleday and Co., Inc., 1981), 174.

p. 64, par. 2, When discussing "*In pace requiescat!*" (671), G. R. Thompson writes that he is not sure "whether the reference is to Fortunato or to himself—or if in fact it is Montresor's utterance at all." *Selected Writings of Edgar Allan Poe* (New York: W. W. Norton and Company, 2004), 421n7.

p. 70, par. 2, Poe's use of mirror images is discussed by critics. For example, *see* Craig Howes, "Teaching 'Usher' and Genre: Poe and the Introductory Literature Class," *The Journal of the Midwest Modern Language Association* 19.1 (Spring 1986), 31–36; and John H. Timmerman, "House of Mirrors: Edgar Allan Poe's 'The Fall of the House of Usher,'" *Papers on Language and Literature* 39.3 (Summer 2003), 235–237.

p. 71, par. 1, Other critics agree with Burduck's assessment that "The Fall of the House of Usher" is one of Poe's finest stories. Arthur Hobson Quinn calls it "one of his very greatest stories." *Edgar Allan Poe: A Critical Biography* (Baltimore: Johns Hopkins University Press, 1998), 284. Vincent Buranelli says the tale "is perhaps the finest thing Poe ever wrote." *Edgar Allan Poe* (New York: Twayne Publishers, 1961), 77.

p. 71, par. 3, Not everyone agrees on the symbolic meaning of the seven rooms in Prince Prospero's castle. G. R. Thompson notes: "One of the favorite pastimes of critics is trying to identify the symbolic meaning of the colors of the seven rooms. Speculation includes the seven ages of man, the seven days of the week, the seven deadly sins, the seven Christian sacraments, and so forth. Some readers have noted that the rooms proceed from east to west, blue at one end and black at the other, suggesting the cycle of a day from night to night." Thompson, ed., *Selected Writings,* 301n3.

p. 76, par. 2, For a good discussion of the characteristics of Poe's detective stories, see Buranelli, *Edgar Allan Poe,* 81–85; and David Van Leer, "Detecting Truth: The World of the Dupin Tales," in *New Essays on Poe's Major Tales,* ed. Kenneth Silverman (New York: Cambridge University Press, 1993), pp. 65–74.

p. 76, par. 3, For a discussion of the structure of the "The Murders in the Rue Morgue," *see* Van Leer, pp. 67–68.

p. 85, par. 2, Another reason that the narrator of "The Tell-Tale Heart" wants to prove his sanity is offered by Christopher Benfey, who explains that the narrator is afraid "of being *cut off*, of being misunderstood." "Poe and the Unreadable: 'The Black Cat' and 'The Tell-Tale Heart,'" in *New Essays*, Silverman, 37.

p. 86, par. 4–p. 87, par. 1, For detailed information concerning Poe's reputation in Europe, *see* Patrick F. Quinn, *The French Face of Edgar Poe* (Carbondale: Southern Illinois University Press, 1957).

Chapter 4
p. 90, par. 1, For a discussion of the literary techniques Poe uses in "Annabel Lee," *see* Floyd Stovall, *Edgar Poe the Poet* (Charlottesville: University Press of Virginia, 1969), 225.

p. 91, par. 4, For a discussion of the literary techniques Poe uses in "The Bells," *see* Stovall, 231–232.

p. 92, par. 1, Kevin Graham believes that Poe, in "The Bells," not only conveys "emotional effects to his readers, but he also makes his readers subconsciously convey those effects with facial expressions when the poem is read aloud" (11). He argues that "When one reads aloud the last line of each stanza of the poem, his or her facial expression reflects the mood the certain type of bell conveys" (10). Thus in the first stanza, the feeling of pleasure is reflected in readers' faces as they read the words "'jingling" and "tinkling" which each have two *ng* and *nk* sounds, "sounds that, when said, almost force the human face to smile, making the reader physically convey the uplifted tone of the stanza" (10). When speaking the last line of the second stanza, speakers are once again forced to look happy because Poe "combines the diphthong [ai] with the palatovelar sound [ng] in the words 'rhyming' and 'chiming,' thereby increasing the size of the smile on the reader's face" (10). Contrarily, readers show pain when reading the final line of verse three as the words "clamor" and "clangor" force them to drop their jaws and open their mouths, making a facial expression "similar to the one made when a person accidentally hits his or her thumb with a hammer" (10). In the stanza on death, readers portray a "cadaverous appearance" when they drop their jaws and protrude their lips to pronounce "moaning" and "groaning." "Poe's 'The Bells,'" *The Explicator* 62.1 (Fall 2003), 10–11.

p. 94, par. 3–p. 95, par. 1, Several authors discuss Poe's use of the word "shadow" in "Eldorado." *See* W. Stephen Sanderlin Jr., "Poe's 'Eldorado' Again," *Modern Language Notes* 71.2 (March 1956), 189; Kenneth Silverman, *Edgar A. Poe* (New York: HarperCollins, 1991), 403; and Stovall, 225.

p. 99, par. 2, For a discussion of the literary techniques Poe uses in "The Raven," *see* Stovall, 226–228.

p. 102, par. 2, Patrick F. Quinn analyzes the French response to Poe. See *The French Face of Edgar Poe* (Carbondale: Southern Illinois University Press, 1957).

Chapter 5
p. 107, par. 1, Shawn James Rosenheim argues that Poe's detective fiction, as well as his science ficiton, the "Marginalia," and *Eureka*, contain cryptographic (secret)

writings, a type of "literature that, in the century and a half since Poe's death, has become increasingly influential" (2). Rosenheim asserts that Poe's influence is felt not only in literature but also in real life by actual cryptographers during World War II and the Cold War, as well as by users of the Internet. (See *The Cryptographic Imagination*, Baltimore: Johns Hopkins University Press, 1997).

p. 108, par. 1, In the late nineteenth and early twentieth centuries, musicians were very interested in Poe's works. In addition to Debussy and Rachmaninoff, Florent Schmitt wrote an étude, *Le palais hante*, based on "The Haunted Palace" in 1904; in 1924, Andre Caplet composed *Conte fantastique* for harp and strings, a work inspired by "The Masque of the Red Death"; English composer Joseph Holbrooke wrote a symphonic poem based on "The Raven" in 1900, a symphonic poem based on "The Bells" in 1903, and a ballet based on "The Masque of the Red Death."

In the late twentieth century, musicians once again looked to Poe for inspiration. Bruce Adolphe of the Chamber Music Society of Lincoln Center in New York City made *The Tell-Tale Heart* into an opera in 1978; minimalist Philip Glass wrote an opera based on "The Fall of the House of Usher" in 1989; choral composer Jonathan Adams set three Poe poems to music in 1993 and "Annabel Lee" in 1995; Augusta Read Thomas's opera *Ligeia* appeared in 1994; and in Finland, Einojuhani Rautavaara in 1997 wrote a fantasia for chorus and orchestra, *On the Last Frontier*, based on *The Narrative of Arthur Gordon Pym*. Further information about the use of Poe by classical musicians can be found at this Web site: "Discover. Exceptional." http://www.amer ican symphony.org/dialogues_extensions/99_2000sea-son1999_10_15 (Accessed August 21, 2007).

p. 108, par. 1, For a more complete list of Poe's influence

on popular music, *see* "Poe's Ultimate Song List," http://www.houseofusher.net/songs/html (Accessed August 21, 2007).

p. 110, par. 1, Much information on Poe's place in popular culture can be found on the Internet. For example, *see* "Poe's Enduring Fame," *Edgar Allan Poe Society of Baltimore*, http://www. eapoe.org (Accessed August 22, 2007).

Further Information

Further Reading

Works by Poe
Poe, Edgar Allan. *The Complete Tales and Poems of Edgar Allan Poe with Selections from His Critical Writings.* Introduction and explanatory notes by Arthur Hobson Quinn. Bibliographical notes by Edward H. O'Neill. New York: Barnes & Noble, 1992.

Ostrom, John Ward, ed. *The Letters of Edgar Allan Poe.* 2 vols. New York: Gordian Press, 1966.

Works About Poe
Kennedy, J. Gerald., ed. *A Historical Guide to Edgar Allan Poe.* Oxford: Oxford University Press, 2001.

Pearl, Matthew. *The Poe Shadow.* New York: Random House, 2006.

Quinn, Arthur Hobson. *Edgar Allan Poe: A Critical Biography.* Baltimore: Johns Hopkins University Press, 1941; reprinted 1998.

Silverman, Kencth. Edgar A. Poe: Mornful and Never-ending Remembrance. New York: HarperCollins, 1991.

Thompson, G. R., ed. *The Selected Writings of Edgar Allan Poe: Authoritative Texts, Backgrounds and Contexts, Criticism.* New York: W. W. Norton & Company, 2004.

Web Sites

About Edgar Allan Poe
http://www.classicauthors.net/Poe/
Contains a timeline of Poe's published works, a list of works that can be read online, a biography, and information on Poe's works.

A Poe Webliography, by Heyward Ehrlich
http://andromeda.rutgers.edu/~ehrlich/poesites.html
Includes a comprehensive online collection of Poe texts.

Bartleby: Edgar Allan Poe
http://www.bartleby.com/people/Poe-Edga.html
A bibliography of Poe's works is listed here. It also has many links to learn about Poe's life.

The Poe Decoder
http://www.poedecoder.com
The Poe Decoder by Christoffer Nilsson and others features criticism and information on Poe and his work.

Poe Society of Baltimore
http://www.eapoe.org
Contains both primary and secondary materials. It has a large number of Poe e-texts as well as surveys of Poe editions, the Poe canon, and discussions on Poe topics.

Bibliography

1. Primary Sources
Poe, Edgar Allan. *The Complete Tales and Poems of Edgar Allan Poe with Selections from His Critical Writings*. Introduction and explanatory notes by Arthur Hobson Quinn. Bibliographical notes by Edward H. O'Neill. New York: Barnes & Noble, 1992.

Ostrom, John Ward, ed. *The Letters of Edgar Allan Poe*. 2 vols. New York: Gordian Press, 1966.

2. Secondary Sources
Aiken, Joan. *Arabel's Raven*. Garden City, NY: Doubleday, 1974.

Alterton, Margaret, and Hardin Craig. *Edgar Allan Poe: Representative Selections* New York: American Book Company, 1935.

Avi. *The Man Who Was Poe: A Novel*. New York: Orchard Books, 1989.

Bailey, J. O. "What Happens in 'The Fall of the House of Usher'?" *American Literature* 35.4 (January, 1964), 445–466.

Baraban, Elena V. "The Motive for Murder in 'The Cask of Amontillado' by Edgar Allan Poe." *Rocky Mountain Review of Language and Literature* 58.2 (2004), 47–62.

Baudelaire, Charles Pierre. "New Notes on Edgar Poe." In Carlson, *Critical Essays*, 63–77.

Benfey, Christopher. "Poe and the Unreadable: 'The Black Cat' and 'The Tell-Tale Heart.'" In Silverman, *New Essays*, 27–44.

Benitez, Dr. R. Michael. "Rabies." *Maryland Medical Journal*, 45 (September 1996), 765–769.

Blair, Walter, et. al. *American Literature: A Brief History.* Rev. ed. Glenview, IL: Scott, Foresman, 1974.

Bloch, Robert. "Foreword." In Haining, *The Edgar Allan Poe Scrapbook*, 6–7.

Bonaparte, Marie. "Morella." In Carlson, *The Recognition*, 172–176.

Bonner, Charles H. *John Pendleton Kennedy; Gentleman from Baltimore.* Baltimore: Johns Hopkins Press, 1961.

Bonner, Thomas Jr. "The Epistolary Poe." A Lecture Delivered at the Edgar Allan Poe Society of Baltimore on October 6, 1996. Baltimore: The Edgar Allan Poe Society and the Library of the University of Baltimore, 2001.

Buranelli, Vincent. *Edgar Allan Poe.* New York: Twayne Publishers, 1961.

Burduck, Michael L. *Usher's 'Forgotten Church'?: Edgar Allan Poe and Nineteenth-Century American Catholicism.* Baltimore, Maryland: Edgar Allan Poe Society and the Library of the University of Baltimore, 2000.

Campbell, Killis. *The Poems of Edgar Allan Poe.* Boston: Ginn and Company, 1917.

Caputi, Anthony. "The Refrain in Poe's Poetry." *American Literature* 25.2 (Mary 1953), 169–178.

Carlson, Eric W., ed. *Critical Essays on Edgar Allan Poe.* Boston: G. K. Hall, 1987.

———. "Poe's 'Eldorado.'" *Modern Language Notes* 76.3 (March 1961), 232–233.

———, ed. *The Recognition of Edgar Allan Poe.* Ann Arbor: University of Michigan Press, 1966.

Clark, Harry Hayden. *Major American Poets.* New York: American Book Company, 1936.

Coad, Oral Sumner. "The Meaning of Poe's 'Eldorado.'" *Modern Language Notes* 59.1 (January 1944), 59–61.

Cooke, P. Pendleton. "Edgar A. Poe." In Carlson, *The Recognition,* 21 28.

Davidson, Edward Hutchins. *Poe, A Critical Study.* Cambridge: Harvard University Press, 1957.

"Discover. Exceptional."http://www.americansymphony. org/dialogues_extensions/99_2000season1999_10_15 (Accessed August 21, 2007).

Duyckinck, Evert Augustus. "Review of *The Works of the Late Edgar Allan Poe* (1850 Griswold Edition)." In Carlson, *Critical Essays,* 50–52.

Eliot, Thomas Stearns. "From Poe to Valéry." In Carlson, *The Recognition,* 205–220.

"*Eureka: A Prose Poem* by Edgar A. Poe." In Carlson, *Critical Essays,* 49–50.

Fletcher, Richard M. *The Stylistic Development of Edgar Allan Poe.* The Hague: Mouton, 1973.

Forgues, E. D. "The Tales of Edgar A. Poe." In Carlson, *Critical Essays*, 41–49.

Freimarck, Vincent and Bernard Rosenthal, eds. *Race and the American Romantics.* New York: Schocken Books, 1971.

Fuller, Margaret. "[Review of *Tales* (1845) by Edgar A. Poe]." *Critical Essays*, 36–37.

———. "[Review of *The Raven and Other Poems* (1845) by Edgar A. Poe]." In Carlson, *Critical Essays*, 38–41.

Gargano, James W. "The Question of Poe's Narrators." In Carlson, *The Recognition*, 308–316.

Gibson, Thomas. "Cadet Poe of West Point." In Haining, *The Edgar Allan Poe Scrapbook*, 52–54.

Godden, Richard. "Poe and the Poetics of Opacity: Or, Another Way of Looking at that Black Bird." *ELH* 67.4 (2000), 993–1009.

Graham, Kevin. "Poe's 'The Bells.'" *The Explicator* 62.1 (Fall 2003), 9–11.

Graves, Charles Marshall. "Landmarks of Poe in Richmond." In Haining, *The Edgar Allan Poe Scrapbook*, 33–38.

Griswold, Rufus Wilmot. "The 'Ludwig' Article." In Carlson, *The Recognition*, 28–35.
———. "[From 'Memoir of the Author']." In Carlson, *Critical Essays on Edgar Allan Poe*, 52–58.

Haining, Peter, ed. *The Edgar Allan Poe Scrapbook*. New York: Schocken Books, 1978.

Harrison, James Albert. *The Life and Letters of Edgar Allan Poe*. Vol. 1. New York: Thomas Y. Crowel & Sons, 1903.

Hatvary, George Egon. *The Murder of Edgar Allan Poe: A Novel*. New York: Carroll & Graf, 1997.

Hayes, Kevin J. *Poe and the Printed Word*. Cambridge: Cambridge University Press, 2000.

Hoffman, Daniel. *Poe Poe Poe Poe Poe Poe Poe*. Baton Rouge: Louisiana State University Press, 1972.

Horton, Rod W. and Herbert W. Edwards. *Backgrounds of American Literary Thought*, 2nd ed. New York: Appleton-Century-Crofts, 1967.

Hovey, Kenneth Alan. "Critical Provincialism: Poe's Poetic Principle in Antebellum Context," *American Quarterly* 39.3 (Autumn 1987), 341–354.

Howarth, William L. ed. *Twentieth Century Interpretations of Poe's Tales: A Collection of Critical Essays*. Englewood Cliffs, NJ: Prentice-Hall, 1971.

Howells, William Dean. "Literary Friends and Acquaintance." In *William Dean Howells: Representative Selections*. Introduction, Bibliography, and Notes by Clara Marburg Kirk and Rudolf Kirk. Rev. ed. New York: Hill and Wang, 1961, 16–69.

Howes, Craig. "Teaching 'Usher' and Genre: Poe and the Introductory Literature Class." *The Journal of the Midwest Modern Language Association* 19.1 (Spring, 1986), 29–42.

Huxley, Aldous Leonard. "Vulgarity in Literature." In Carlson, *The Recognition*, 160–167.

Ingram, John H. *Edgar Allan Poe: His Life, Letters, and Opinions*. New York: Ams Press, 1965.

Irwin, John T. *The Mystery to a Solution: Poe, Borges, and the Analytic Detective Story*. Baltimore: Johns Hopkins University Press, 1994.

James, Henry. "Comments." In Carlson, *The Recognition of Edgar Allan Poe*, 65–67.

Kaplan, Louise J. "The Perverse Strategy in 'The Fall of the House of Usher.'" In Silverman, *New Essays*, 45–64.

Kennedy, J. Gerald., ed. *A Historical Guide to Edgar Allan Poe*. Oxford: Oxford University Press, 2001.

King, Stephen, and Peter Straub. *Black House: A Novel*. New York: Random House, 2001.

King, Stephen. *Insomnia*. New York: Viking, 1994.

Lawrence, D. H. "Edgar Allan Poe." In Carlson, *Critical Essays*, 91–102.

Levine, Stuart. *Edgar Poe: Seer and Craftsman*. Deland, FL: Everett/Edwards, 1972.

"The Literary Mohawk." In Haining, *The Edgar Allan Poe Scrapbook*, 79.
Lowell, James Russell. "Edgar Allan Poe." In Carlson, *The Recognition*, 5–17.

Mabbott, Thomas Ollive. "The Sources of Poe's 'Eldorado.'" *Modern Language Notes* 60.5 (May 1945), 312–314.

Malloy, Jeanne M. "Apocalyptic Imagery and the Fragmentation of the Psyche: 'The Pit and the Pendulum.'" *Nineteenth-Century Literature* 46.1 (June 1991), 82–95.

Matthiessen, F. O. *American Renaissance; Art and Expression in the Age of Emerson and Whitman.* London: Oxford University Press, 1941.

May, Charles. *Edgar Allan Poe: A Study of the Short Fiction.* Boston: Twayne, 1991.

Miller, John Carl. *Building Poe Biography.* Baton Rouge: Louisiana State University Press, 1977.

Moss, Sidney P. *Poe's Literary Battles: The Critic in the Context of His Literary Milieu.* Durham, NC: Duke University Press, 1963.

Nabokov, Vladimir Vladimirovich. *Lolita.* Paris: Olympia Press, 1955.

National Park Service. *Teacher's Handbook: Edgar Allan Poe National Historic Site.* National Park Service: U.S. Department of the Interior, n.d.

Neal, John. "Comments on Poe's Poems." *Yankee and Boston Literary Gazette*, September/December 1829. In Carlson, *The Recognition of Edgar Allan Poe*, 3–4.

Pearl, Matthew. *The Poe Shadow.* New York: Random House, 2006.

Peeples, Scott. *Edgar Allan Poe Revisited.* New York: Twayne, 1998.

Peithman, Stephen. "The Cask of Amontillado." In *The Annotated Tales of Edgar Allan Poe*. Ed. Stephen Peithman. Garden City, NY: Doubleday and Co., Inc., 1981, 168–174.

Perowne, Barry. *A Singular Conspiracy*. Indianapolis: Bobbs-Merrill, 1974.

"Poe's Enduring Fame." *Edgar Allan Poe Society of Baltimore*, http://www.eapoe.org (Accessed August 22, 2007).

"Poe's Ultimate Song List." http://www.houseofusher. net/songs/html (Accessed August 21, 2007).

Pritchard, Hollie. "Poe's 'The Tell-Tale Heart.'" *The Explicator* 61.3 (Spring 2003), 144–147.

Quinn, Arthur Hobson. *Edgar Allan Poe: A Critical Biography*. Baltimore: Johns Hopkins University Press, 1941; reprinted 1998.

Quinn, Patrick F. *The French Face of Edgar Poe* Carbondale: Southern Illinois University Press, 1957.

Reynolds, David S. "Poe's Art of Transformation: 'The Cask of Amontillado' in Its Cultural Context." In Silverman, *New Essays*, 93–112.

Richards, Eliza. "Outsourcing 'The Raven': Retroactive Origins." *Victorian Poetry* 43.2 (Summer 2005), 205–221.

Robinson, E. Arthur. "Poe's 'The Tell-Tale Heart.'" *Nineteenth-Century Fiction* 19.4 (March 1965), 369–378.

Roderick, Phillip, L. *The Fall of the House of Poe and Other Essays*. New York: iUniverse, 2006.

Rosenheim, Shawn James. *The Cryptographic Imagination.* Baltimore: Johns Hopkins University Press, 1997.

Rosenthal, Bernard. "Poe, Slavery, and the *Southern Literary Messenger*: A Reexamination." *Poe Studies* 7 (December 1974), 29–38.

Rucker, Rudy. *The Hollow Earth: The Narrative of Mason Algiers Reynolds of Virginia.* New York: W. Morrow, 1990.

Sanderlin, W. Stephen Jr. "Poe's 'Eldorado' Again." *Modern Language Notes* 71.2 (March 1956), 189–192.

Schechter, Harold. *The Hum Bug: A Novel.* New York: Pocket Books, 2001.

———. *The Mask of Red Death: An Edgar Allan Poe Mystery.* New York: Ballantine Books, 2004.

———. *Nevermore: A Novel.* New York: Pocket Books, 1999.

———. *The Tell-Tale Corpse: An Edgar Allan Poe Mystery.* New York: Ballantine Books, 2006.

Shaw, George Bernard. "Edgar Allan Poe." In Carlson, *Critical Essays*, 86–91.

Silverman, Kenneth. *Edgar A. Poe: Mournful and Never-ending Remembrance.* New York: HarperCollins, 1991.

———, ed. *New Essays on Poe's Major Tales.* New York: Cambridge University Press, 1993.

Smith, C. Alphonso. "Our Heritage of Idealism." *Sewanee Review* 20 (April 1912), 248–249.

Stovall, Floyd. *Edgar Poe the Poet: Essays New and Old on the Man and His Work.* Charlottesville: University Press of Virginia, 1969.

Swinburne, Algernon Charles. "Letter to Sara Sigourney Rice." In Carlson, *Critical Essays*, 79–80.

Tasistro, Louis Fitzgerald. "A Notice of Poe's Tales." In Carlson, *The Recognition*, 4–5.

Tate, Allen. "The Angelic Imagination." In Carlson, *The Recognition*, 236–254.

Taylor, Andrew. *An Unpardonable Crime.* New York: Theia, 2004.

Thomas, Dwight and David K. Jackson. *The Poe Log: A Documentary Life of Edgar Allan Poe 1809–1849.* Boston: G. K. Hall, 1987.

Thompson, G. R. *Poe's Fiction: Romantic Irony in the Gothic Tales.* Madison, WI: University of Wisconsin Press, 1973.

———, ed. *The Selected Writings of Edgar Allan Poe: Authoritative Texts, Backgrounds and Contexts, Criticism.* New York: W. W. Norton & Company, 2004.

Timmerman, John H. "House of Mirrors: Edgar Allan Poe's 'The Fall of the House of Usher.'" *Papers on Language and Literature* 39.3 (Summer 2003), 227–244.

Tucker, T. G. "The University Story-Teller." In Haining, *The Edgar Allan Poe Scrapbook*, 39–40.

Tupper, Martin Farquhar. "American Romance." In Carlson, *The Recognition*, 18–21.

Van Leer, David. "Detecting Truth: The World of the Dupin Tales." In Silverman, *New Essays*, 65–92.

Weiner, Bruce I. "The Most Noble of Professions: Poe and the Poverty of Authorship." A Lecture Given at the Edgar Allan Poe Society of Baltimore on October 5, 1986. Baltimore: Enoch Pratt Free Library, the Edgar Allan Poe Society, and the Library of the University of Baltimore, 1987.

Whalen, Terence. "Poe and the American Publishing Industry." In Kennedy, *A Historical Guide to Edgar Allan Poe*, 63–93.

———. *Poe and the Masses: The Political Economy of Literature in Antebellum America*. Princeton, NJ: Princeton University Press, 1999.

Whitman, Walt. "Edgar Poe's Significance." In Carlson, *Critical Essays*, 83–85.

Wilbur, Richard. "The House of Poe." In Carlson, *The Recognition*, 254–277.

———. "Poe and the Art of Suggestion." In Carlson, *Critical Essays*, 160–171.

Wilson, Edmund. "Poe as a Literary Critic." In Carlson, *Critical Essays*, 109–113.

Winters, Yvor. "Edgar Allan Poe: A Crisis in the History of American Obscurantism." In Carlson, *The Recognition*, 176–202.

Yeats, William Butler. "Letter to W. T. Horton, Sept. 3, 1899." In Carlson, *The Recognition*, 76–77.

Index

Page numbers in **boldface** are illustrations, tables, and charts.
Proper names of fictional characters are shown by (C).

About the Author

RAYCHEL HAUGRUD REIFF, a professor of English at the University of Wisconsin-Superior, has published articles on literary topics and effective teaching techniques in various journals and books. Her most recent book in Marshall Cavendish Benchmark's Writers and Their Works series is *Sylvia Plath: The Bell Jar and Poems*. She lives in Superior, Wisconsin.